G000292709

LET'S SIGN

By the same author

SIGNS MAKE SENSE: A Guide to British Sign Language
Souvenir Press
SIGN IN SIGHT: A Step into the Deaf World
Souvenir Press
SIGN LANGUAGE COMPANION: A Handbook of British Signs
Souvenir Press

FROM CO-SIGN COMMUNICATIONS

SIGN LANGUAGE LINK: A Pocket Dictionary of Signs

SIGNS OF HEALTH: A Pocket Medical Sign Language Guide

SIGN LANGUAGE LINK: Desk Edition

THE LET'S SIGN SERIES

LET'S SIGN: BSL Building Blocks Student Primer

LET'S SIGN: BSL Greetings Signs and Fingerspelling Wallchart (A2)

LET'S SIGN: A4 Poster/Mats Set 1
Greetings-Family-Feelings-Questions

LET'S SIGN: A4 Bildtafeln zur
Deutschen Gebärdensprache
Tätigkeiten - Familie - Fragen - Gefühle

LET'S SIGN: For Work

LET'S SIGN: Early Years

LET'S SIGN & WRITE: BSL Graphics for Sign Bilingual Materials

LET'S SIGN:

BSL Building Blocks Tutor

Written and Illustrated by

CATH SMITH

CO-SIGN COMMUNICATIONS

Copyright © 2001 by Cath Smith

The right of Cath Smith to be identified as author of this work has been asserted by her in accordance with the Copyright, Designs and Patents Act 1988.

First published 2001 Reprinted 2004

ISBN 0 9535069 3 2

All rights reserved. No part of this publication may be reproduced, stored in a retrieval system, or transmitted, in any form or by any means, electronic, mechanical, photocopying, recording or otherwise without the prior permission of the Copyright owner.

Published by Co-Sign Communications,
Stockton-on-Tees, TS18 5HH
Tel: 01642 580505 Fax: 01642 808959
email: cath@deafsign.com   www.deafsign.com

Distributed by Forest Books,
The New Building, Ellwood Road, Milkwall,
Coleford, Gloucestershire GL16 7LE
Tel: 01594 833858 Fax: 01594 833446
email: forest@forestbooks.com
www.ForestBooks.com

Typesetting and Layout by
Robert Riley, Yarm, Stockton on Tees

Printed in Great Britain by Alphabet Press,
17 Southview, Bear Park, Durham DH7 7DE

FOREWORD

Minister for the Cabinet Office
Chancellor of the Duchy of Lancaster

"Cath Smith's 'Let's Sign' provides a great introduction to sign language
and will be of huge help to those who are wanting to learn how to communicate.

The book is clear, professional, simple to understand and easy to learn from and I
have no hesitation in recommending it."

Mo

Marjorie Mowlam

ACKNOWLEDGEMENTS

My grateful thanks and appreciation for;

Help and advice in the early stages of planning this project, from;
Mr Jack Goodfellow, Advisor, Advisory Service in Education,
Education, Leisure and Cultural Services Department, Stockton-on-Tees.
Marian Wright, Literacy Consultant, Education Centre, Stockton-on-Tees.
Margaret Whelan, Primary School Teacher, Middlesbrough.
Lynn Simpson, Child and Adolescent Mental Health Service, Peterlee.
Sandra Teasdale, Peripatetic Teaching Support Worker, Hearing Impaired Service,
Middlesbrough.

Feedback and comments on the sign illustrations, contents and format;
Angie, Paul and Amy Beckett, Redcar.
Joan Hughes, Bobby Shaftoe's Play Group, Community Centre, Satlburn.

Technical support;
Tony Huck, Tony Elsdon and Colin Robson.

Preparing the book for publication;
Robert Riley, Yarm, typesetting and layout.
Peter Moon, Stockton-on-Tees, sounding board.
Patricia Farrell, Chandler's Ford, support and advice.
Graham Canwell, Middlesbrough, cover design.
Wendy Finnegan, Northallerton, proof reading.
Stephen Smith, Durham, printing.

A special thank you to the Right Honourable Dr. Marjorie (Mo) Mowlam MP for
kindly agreeing to see a draft copy of the book and giving it her approval.

To my husband David and son William
who can look forward to using the computer again.

CONTENTS

PREFACE

Since this **Let's Sign Taster pack** was first published in 2001, we have developed it into a series of resources that can be used together to support teaching and learning. Full details have been added at the end of this edition.

This pack is available through Curriculum Online.

The **Let's Sign** Student Primer is available to accompany this Tutor. It is designed to accompany the lessons, worksheets, exercises and games from the Tutor, giving students a handy reference book of the signs for class or home work. It is strongly recommended that the two books and CD-Rom are used together.

At the eleventh hour before publication, we put together the idea of producing the CD-Rom to provide moving video clip images of the signs in the book. With thanks to our web designers Interactive Net Solutions who made the suggestions, and a Match Funded Marketing Grant from the Environment and Technical Services Department, Stockton-on-Tees Borough Council, and further assistance from The Ropner Trust, Stockton-on-Tees, we made the CD-Rom.

My sincere thanks go to Angie, Paul and Amy Beckett for so kindly agreeing to be involved. I have known Angie and Paul since they were deaf children themselves, when my social worker with deaf people role brought me into contact with their hearing families, then through my work as Communication Tutor and Interpreter at the deaf school they attended.

At the time of filming in January 2001, Amy is three and a half years old. Amy is one of less than 10% of deaf children born to deaf parents, and is fortunate to have a natural first language through BSL - acquired in the home - just as other children acquire their mother tongue. English will be Amy's second language. Amy will be educated at a local mainstream school with support from the Hearing Impaired Service.

Angie and Paul want Amy to be treated just like any other child. They do not view Amy's, or their own deafness, as a disability, but as a difference.

We hope that **Let's Sign** will encourage pupils, teachers and others who have contact with deaf people and children to have better understanding of deafness and communication.

Let's Sign can be further built on and developed according to need and your comments and feedback are greatly valued.

PLEASE CONTACT US AT

Co-Sign Communications, 16 Highfield Crescent, Hartburn, Stockton-on-Tees, TS18 5HH Tel: 01642 580505 Fax: 01642 808959 email: cath@deafsign.com

Visit our NGfL approved and Schoolzone 5 star rated website
www.deafsign.com

Cath Smith March 2001 and February 2004

INTRODUCTION
Why Learn BSL (British Sign Language)?

Learning any language is a new adventure that some people take to more easily than others. Learning sign language - in this case British Sign Language, the language of Britain's Deaf community, is an even greater adventure, as it uncovers different cultural perspectives and unexpected controversies.

Learning about the language involves learning about its background and significance to the lives of the people who use it. BSL has a history of oppression that has had profound consequences for generations of Deaf people, bringing a determination that history should not be allowed to repeat itself.

Disregarding the label of disability, most members of the Deaf community regard themselves as part of a cultural linguistic minority. One of the chief defining features of culture and identity is language and *Deaf people have been calling for the official recognition of BSL for many years.

BSL is a visual gestural language that uses a different medium to the spoken language we are accustomed to, and this also brings with it some surprises that we may not be expecting.

Growing numbers of people are keen to learn more about sign language and the Deaf community who use it, and wish they'd had the opportunity to do this in their school years.

People of any age can learn sign language, but childhood is undoubtably the best time for language learning. Not only is a new language easier to acquire in childhood, but signs also bring a multi-sensory component that can benefit all children's conceptual development, memory, and literacy skills. For these reasons, ironic though it is after decades of controversy over its use in deaf education, sign language now seems to be gaining interest in mainstream schools and society.

Let's Sign offers a new approach to learning and teaching BSL that focuses on the formation of the signs themselves as a starting point rather than their English translations. (This important distinction was pioneered by the British Deaf Association's Dictionary of British Sign Language/English, see Sources).

Beginning with an introductory overview and background that covers the role and importance of BSL to Deaf people and children, it leads on to introducing BSL in a structured way.

Through the components of the face and body, the handshapes, locations and movements which form the Building Blocks, signs are constructed in handshape groups to form a useful basic core vocabulary that learners of all ages can relate to. The signs chosen include *social* and *emotional concepts* that should also complement programmes aimed at developing **social** and **interpersonal competence** and **emotional literacy**. The materials offer something for all ages and all abilities

There are 5 basic handshapes with sets of 10 signs each, plus 10 extra conversational signs making 60 in total. The signs are presented in a variety of styles and formats to make learning and teaching easier, more enjoyable and hopefully more effective.

*The convention of the upper case 'D' in Deaf is used in this book to identify culturally Deaf sign language users.

Who Can Use 'Let's Sign'?

95% of deaf youngsters are now in mainstream schools. For schools attended by deaf children – whether their hearing loss is profound or partial, there is an even more urgent need for fellow class-mates to be **'Deaf Aware'** and able to communicate clearly, if the deaf child or children are to be included in any meaningful way.

There have been examples in the media of entire school populations joining in and learning sign language, making a real difference to the deaf child's self esteem and identity.

More importantly, the chance to foster open-minded attitudes to different cultures and modes of communication is never better than with young children – forming attitudes that can stay with us for life. More people learning sign language, means a better chance of equality and integration for deaf people and children in the future.

This can be in:

MAINSTREAM SCHOOLS

- To foster the inclusion of deaf children and enable incidental learning

- To improve language and communication skills generally

- As part of the Citizenship curriculum

- To add a new dimension to Literacy Hour, Circle Time, and Assemblies

- With social and interpersonal competence and emotional literacy programmes

- To teach sight vocabulary for reading and improve spelling

FAMILIES OF DEAF CHILDREN
Parents and extended family members, particularly grandparents whose needs are often overlooked.

BSL BEGINNERS COURSES
As a general introduction and ice-breaker games and exercises.

OLDER DEAFENED AND HARD OF HEARING LEARNERS
Who may wish to learn some basic signs and fingerspelling to supplement communication.

CHILDREN AND ADULTS WITH LEARNING DIFFICULTIES AND SPECIAL NEEDS
May benefit from the structured approach and clear instructions. The worksheets and games are suitable for a wide range of abilities.

CHILDREN AND YOUNG PEOPLE'S GROUPS
Brownies, Guides, Beavers, Cubs, Scouts.
Leaders can integrate the learning of BSL into regular weekly sessions.

Frequently Asked Questions

Can deaf people lip-read?

Yes and no. This is a huge area that deserves a book in itself, but is such a common assumption that it needs some mention. The use of lip-reading as a totally adequate and reliable substitute for hearing speech is very rare indeed. To be able to pick up word patterns from the mouth requires that you are familiar with the words, phrases, figures of speech and so on, in the first place. For people who are hearing and become deaf after spoken language development, lip-reading can be an enormous help. Most people can lip-read to a certain extent and you only have to hear the complaints after televised football matches to learn which speech patterns are the easiest to lip-read. 'F', 'W' and 'B' provide lovely clear patterns, but 'F' also looks like 'V', 'W' like 'QU' and 'B' like both 'M' and 'P', (try mouthing *ban, man* and *pan* in the mirror) so that context and guesswork play a huge part. For people who are born deaf and who are not familiar with many spoken words, it is much more limited, but with familiar words and in context is still useful.

Do all deaf people use sign language?

Not at all. The largest group of deaf people - the estimated 8,700,000 people, who have lost all or part of their hearing after spoken language and a hearing identity have been established, are likely to retain their hearing identity and use of speech/lipreading/writing as their main means of communication. Their spoken language will be their first language, even if they never hear again. People who are deaf from birth or early childhood however, form the nucleus of the Deaf community, using the convention of the upper case 'D' in Deaf to identify themselves as culturally Deaf community members and sign language users. This is not merely a preference for sign over spoken language but something that is both essential and greatly valued within the community.

Is sign language universal?

Popular though the notion is, there isn't a universal sign language. Sign languages are certainly used world wide, wherever groups of deaf people and children come together, but they are not all the same language. They share the same building blocks and spatial structures of visual gestural languages which gives them more in common with each other than with spoken languages, but they each have their own rules and vocabularies.

Is BSL standardised?

BSL, like spoken language, has evolved through the needs of its users in spontaneous and natural ways. There are wide regional differences in some signs - numbers and colours are notoriously variable, however most signs are the same. Many of the variations stem from the schools Deaf people attended; new signs are being coined, and more established signs changing with time and use. Hearing learners may find this a problem in the early stages, but it doesn't present a problem to native signers. Variations are largely in the vocabulary of signs - the 'words' of the language; the grammatical structures that hold it together and give meaning, vary very little. Language has a life of its own, and attempts to interfere or control it tend to fail.

Is sign language taught in schools?

Generally speaking, no, although there are some ad hoc classes up and down the country. BSL is not offered as a language option at GCSE level. Some deaf schools now teach sign language and Deaf studies - but not all. Some local authority areas have a policy of 'oral' only communication (speech, aided hearing, lipreading) and exclude sign language altogether leaving families with no choice in these matters.

Can deaf people drive?

Yes they can, and have careers, go to college, university, own their own homes, marry, raise children, and lots of other things along the way.

Do deaf people rely on their eyes more than hearing people?

Vision is clearly important to deaf people. Eye contact and adequate lighting are prerequisites for visual communication. Hearing people need to be more visually aware in Deaf people's company, avoiding visual distractions, and not walking in front of people who are signing. Talking without attempting to sign in Deaf people's company is also considered rude. Getting attention may involve tapping on the shoulder, or arm, or waving the hand slightly in the Deaf person's line of vision. In group gatherings, it can involve flashing the lights briefly on and off. Deaf people generally have been found to have a higher incidence of sight problems compared with the general population. However, deaf people are usually more visually clued in than hearing people. Research has shown that Deaf mothers have a way of communicating visually with their babies and children involving much more use of movement and space (hearing mothers tend to play more with speech and sound). This helps to lay the foundations for visual language development - particularly eye contact and attention.

Do deaf people have deaf children?

Less than 10% of the children born to Deaf parents will also be deaf. Most deaf children - around 90%, are born to hearing couples who may never have encountered deafness before and have no knowledge of sign language. Hearing parents may be devastated to discover that their child is deaf, a reaction that Deaf people find difficult to understand. Deaf people generally value their language and community and most would view having a deaf child in the family quite differently - a reaction that hearing people in turn find strange. Most Deaf people (85 -90%) choose Deaf partners because they share so much through their language and cultural identity, but about 90% of their children will be hearing. Deafness caused by childhood illness, trauma or maternal rubella, is not passed on genetically.

Will signing stop my deaf child from speaking?

This is a common assumption that is even shared by some professionals. Like all children, deaf children have the ability to take from and use language according to need. A bi-lingual option ensures that deaf children have the opportunity to develop signed and spoken language, and can use either to meet their needs in different situations and at different stages. This does not mean speaking and signing at the same time, although this is a commonly used pidgin form of contact language, but using the two languages separately. Early language development is the crucial factor for all children, deaf or hearing, and children should have access to a language that is natural for them and that can be acquired with ease, just as we all acquire a native language. It is not a matter of choosing one language over another, or one method in preference to another method, but of respecting two separate languages and making both visual and spoken language accessible.

A Brief History of BSL - A Story of Oppression

British Sign Language is now usually referred to in its abbreviated form of BSL, just as the sign languages of other countries are referred to in a shortened version, for example, ASL - American Sign Language, AUSlan - Australian Sign Language, DGS - Deutsche Gebärdensprache (German Sign Language) and so on.

As recently as 20 years ago, the term BSL was not yet in regular use, and the sign language of Britain's Deaf Community was regarded as an inferior system of pantomime and gesture that was not a true language. Parents were advised not to allow their children to use signs or even gesture, as this would spoil their chances of developing speech and lipreading skills (this misinformation is still given by some professionals) in spite of the fact that this system was failing the majority of deaf children.

A study carried out in 1979 found that most deaf school leavers had not progressed beyond a reading age of 8.75 years.   In addition, speech quality was found to be largely unintelligible, and skill at lipreading was found to be no better than inexperienced hearing children, dispelling the myth that deaf people are good lipreaders.

Large numbers of adult Deaf people remember vividly, and often with anger, their frustration at not being able to understand what was going on, or to express themselves through sign language.

Neither was sign language used at home, since 90% of deaf children are born into hearing families who have usually never encountered deafness or sign language before. Even when families decided for themselves to offer their children something more, and to learn sign language, classes were virtually non-existent and there were precious few resources on the subject (the authoritative British Deaf Association's Dictionary of British Sign Language was not published until 1992).

Many people are surprised when they discover that sign language was forbidden in deaf education, and not used in the teaching of deaf children until the early 1980's (and even then not in all schools). Its use was discouraged even informally, although deaf children could not be deterred from signing with each other in the playground or when teacher was not looking, since visual language is so essential to them.

The language continues to evolve and be passed on by deaf users. The 10% or so of deaf children of Deaf parents, who develop BSL as a first language, play an important part in this process, as they form the core of a very small number with native language competence.

Deaf adult role models have also been rare in deaf children's lives, to the extent that some deaf children believed that they would no longer be deaf when they grew up, because all the adults they knew were hearing. It was not considered appropriate to employ Deaf people in deaf schools until schools started to adopt policies using sign language, and there are still very few Deaf teachers.

Even today, deaf children may not have adult Deaf contact unless this is specifically sought after and arranged - something that is not always encouraged by the medical profession or educationalists who are the first line of contact for families. The shared knowledge of what it's like to be a deaf child in a hearing world, and the visual language expertise of the adult Deaf community is still rarely passed on to the next generation of deaf children.

Changing Attitudes

Due to research in America in the 1950's and 60's then in Britain during the 1970's and 80's, attitudes towards sign language started to change. Sign languages started to be recognised as full, complex visual languages with structure and grammar very different from spoken languages.

It is now recognised that sign languages exist throughout the world, wherever groups of deaf people and children come together, and each has its own unique vocabulary and rules, although being visual spatial languages, they have a great deal in common with each other - more in common with each other than with spoken languages.

Researchers found that the structures of sign language are different to those used in spoken language for a reason.

In sign language, the physical movement of signs is slow compared to the speed of spoken words. Words can be spoken at roughly double the rate at which signs can be produced, yet it is possible to convey the same meaning and content in the same space of time (this can be seen in simultaneous interpretation from one language to the other). How this happens is really quite ingenious. Sign language relies less on 'words' and more on inventive three dimensional use of space and movement, the brain's answer to our language needs in a different modality.

This allows compacting of detail into signs in an economical way, compensating for slower production since the eye can take it all in at the same time. The reason that this is so important to understand is because these advantages can be lost or distorted when people use signs and speech at the same time.

During the 1980's, training became available for Deaf people to become tutors of their own language. For the first time, courses and examinations in BSL came into being through the formation of the Council for the Advancement of Communication with Deaf People.

Now growing numbers of the general public can be taught BSL by fluent native users of the language, and this has had a big influence on perceptions and understanding of BSL and the Deaf community.

However, many educational policies, usually made by non-Deaf people, continue to promote spoken language only or sign systems that support oral communication but lack the visual grammar of BSL. Deaf children's linguistic needs may still not be met, making it difficult for them to reach their full potential.

The arguments for promoting spoken language over sign language can be persuasive to parents who are vulnerable, find sign language alien and difficult to learn, and are often desperate for their children to speak. There is also the tantalising prospect of never quite knowing with many deaf children if speech will be a realistic option for them or not. There is a real need to meet and talk to Deaf people.

The fact that most deaf children are now in mainstream schools, without signing deaf peers, makes it even more important for schools to de-stigmatise BSL by keeping open minded attitudes, and introduce it into the curriculum for all children.

There is still a long way to go before there is agreement that deaf children need both BSL and English for healthy growth and development and participation in society, but gaining the interest of hearing students, and involving Deaf people have to be the best way forward.

Deaf Children And Communication Needs

Socially and linguistically Deaf people and children come in all shapes and sizes, with diverse needs and abilities that require flexible communication strategies. Many of the Deaf adults who form the Deaf community and use sign language have been through the system of deaf education known as 'oralism', as described in the brief history.

As deaf children, they were not allowed to use sign language in school, and their families were discouraged from using even basic gestures. This was done in the belief that deaf children would not try to speak if they were allowed to sign, that they would rely on signs and not make the effort. Spoken language was, and still is in many quarters, seen as the only language of importance. The system failed many deaf children and some educators began to see the value of sign language.

This subject is still controversial, even to this day, and yet there is no reason why there should be such debate about choosing one language over another. **Both** languages can benefit deaf children's education. The fact that sign language is now thought to improve hearing children's education might just be the spur needed for BSL to be taught in schools.

Deaf people tend to switch modes as they interface with the hearing world and combine lipreading, speech and signs so that a useful **pidgin contact language** has developed. Since BSL and English have quite different structures, this book recommends a **bilingual approach**, which respects the integrity of both languages by keeping them separate (not speaking and signing at the same time). As adult learners, however, many families and teachers may have limited aptitude for languages. Communication and adaptability are the important issues.

Deaf children and mental health

According to the work of the Pathfinder National Deaf Services at Springfield Hospital, London, deaf children are at greater risk of mental health problems. There does not appear to be an increased rate of mental illness for deaf children, but emotional and behavioural problems are between one and a half and twice the rate found in equivalent hearing groups. The main reasons appear to be; communication differences; peer difficulties; higher rates of abuse; higher rates of additional disabilities. Estimates of the prevalence of additional disabilities vary from 15 - 30%.

Some families may be actively discouraged from using any form of signing. Adult classes for BSL rarely cater for the needs of parents learning to communicate with their children. Effective and accessible support in learning BSL may be the exception rather than the rule.   As a result, limitations and difficulties of communication within families are common. Most families of deaf children do manage to find their own way to form meaningful relationships with their child, but an estimated 81% never learn to communicate effectively.

In mainstream schools many deaf children can be isolated from hearing peers, even rejected and bullied and are thought to be at greater risk of abuse generally in view of the obvious difficulties around disclosing. Even in deaf schools, there are no statutory requirements for specialist teachers of the deaf to have any competence in BSL. The same applies to specialist social workers with deaf people.

Some Important Points To Remember

- All children, deaf or hearing can benefit from learning sign language
- Deaf people and children are ideal role models in sign language use
- Basic signs can be learned at any age and by all abilities
- If language is not acquired early, it may never fully develop
- Signed and spoken language are different languages
- Each can improve the acquisition of the other, in spite of the myths that signing impedes speech development, or the acquisition of English
- Deaf children have major weaknesses in spoken language development
- Nearly 50% of profoundly deaf children cannot read for meaning
- Bilingualism in BSL and English give children access to both the Deaf and Hearing world
- Deaf children need both languages for healthy growth and development

Some Facts And Figures On Deafness In Britain

Figures vary. There is no formal measurement of deafness leading to a central registration system in this country as there is with blindness.

There are an estimated **8,700,000 people with hearing loss** (or 1 in 7 of the population) and approximately **60,000 people who are deaf from birth or early childhood** (about 1 per 1,000 of the population), who use sign language and form the British Deaf community.

Some figures on childhood deafness

There are between 23,000 and 25,000 children with permanent hearing loss in this country from birth to 15 years of age.

Many more have temporary loss of hearing in early childhood.

Of those with permanent deafness, about 16,000 were born deaf or became deaf in the first few years of life, before language development and have particular educational needs.

About half of them - 8,000 - are severely or profoundly deaf.

The rate of early childhood deafness - 13 in every 10,000 children - has stayed about the same for the last 20 years.

Although vaccination programmes have reduced the numbers of babies born deaf as a result of their mothers having German measles (rubella) during pregnancy, there are more babies born deaf from other causes.

THE BUILDING BLOCKS OF BSL

The earlier and somewhat dismissive assumption that sign language is merely the use of gestures to make visual representation of events has some truth, in that all sign languages have an element of visual imagery, particularly when new signs are coined. This is likely to evolve and change with use, although some signs, like TREE and BUTTERFLY (not illustrated) become part of the established lexicon, having kept their visual imagery.

Researchers use the term *fixed* or *established* lexicon to refer to signs that function in a similar way to words in spoken language such as may be found in a dictionary or book of sign vocabulary, but these are only part of the story. Sign language also has an enormous degree of creativity and flexibility.

Students frequently ask the question 'what is the sign for….' And, because of their experience of spoken languages, constantly look for word equivalents in BSL. However, as described earlier, sign languages tend to be more flexible, inventive and less word based than spoken languages, allowing users to create signs on the spot, as they are needed.

This is not just random mime and gesture, but involves consistent use of the **building blocks of BSL** to produce meaningful combinations that may be unique to that situation and never used before. Sign language, just like spoken language, has infinite creative possibilities from a finite number of components.

By identifying and understanding the individual components and how these can be combined to give meaning enables new constructions to be made. This is how children acquire language and is how all learners can develop their language skills.

The chief components of these building blocks are;

• the **HANDSHAPES**

• the **PLACEMENT** or **LOCATION** of those handshapes in space or on the head, face or body

• combined with the specific **ORIENTATION/DIRECTION**

• and type of **MOVEMENT**

Added to these manual factors are the **NON-MANUAL FEATURES** of the head, face and body which can add or change meaning, to show, for example, the difference between

• a statement and a question

• to show degree or intensity or

• to change a positive statement into a negative

Deaf people's way of relating to the world involves a visuality - a different conceptual base that hearing people may not be used to and need to clue into.

This section of BSL Building Blocks looks in detail at the individual components, and the signs themselves in the handshape groups. The following page describes these in more detail and makes suggestions for use.

Introducing The Building Blocks

It is recommended wherever possible to involve Deaf people at some stage to help with sign demonstration. Deaf children can also have a responsibility in this area although most will also be in the process of learning BSL themselves.

The information in the **BSL BUILDING BLOCKS** section provides explanations of how signs are constructed from the basic components of facial expressions, handshapes, movements and locations. Once the basic principles are understood and integrated, they can be used and reused in new constructions. Children in particular have a knack of applying rules of language in creative ways.

The worksheets and games in the Materials section provide activities to familiarise students with the building blocks and to apply their knowledge in different contexts to develop spelling and use reading strategies.

Introducing Amy and Ben brings in the two characters who will demonstrate the signs throughout the book. This page shows examples of signs and fingerspelling. The first word signed is 'hello' and Amy and Ben have their own way of signing this, giving the first example of sign variations that students need to clue into. More examples are given in VARIATIONS.

How We Feel focuses on the importance of facial expression. Children may not always be aware of what their faces show, or that adults have feelings too. The worksheets can provide a focus for a range of work on expressing and describing feelings of self and others. This work can be continued and developed as the signs are worked through, using the sign illustrations to develop discussion and/or written work.

For example, the signs SORRY, or PLEASED can be discussed along the lines of

'Ben is **sorry** because he...............' or 'Amy was **pleased** when...............'

And for written work such as *Ben looks sorry, Ben says "sorry, but I........." or Amy is pleased, Amy says " I'm pleased that......."*

It's Not What You Sign....shows some simple examples of how the facial expression can change the meaning of a sign. This is crucial to BSL and sometimes gets overlooked by students in the early stages, when all the concentration seems to be on the hands.

When working through the signs, ask students to try and change the meaning of some of the signs by changing their facial expression. For example, YOU, or ME can be signed as a statement or a question. CROSS, MAD or FURIOUS can be signed with increasing intensity. LIKE can become DON'T LIKE, BROKEN can become NOT BROKEN and so on.

The HANDSHAPES, LOCATION and MOVEMENT pages plus the HANDSHAPE GROUPS and VARIATIONS all come with TUTOR'S NOTES to give more detailed explanation which can be passed on to students as the sign groups are introduced.

Students need to be encouraged to think more visually and view BSL as a separate language, that is not word based in the same way as English. Children are linguistic sponges and good habits can be established from the very beginning.

INTRODUCING AMY AND BEN

Meet Amy and Ben. Amy and Ben will show you how to make the signs. Sometimes they are happy and sometimes they are sad, or cross or puzzled, but they are here to help you learn.

Hello, my name is Amy

Hello, my name is Ben

© 2001 Cath Smith.   May be copied for use by purchaser only.

HOW WE FEEL - WHAT OUR FACES SHOW

Our faces can show the way we feel, even though we may not know it. How do Amy and Ben feel?   Can you write it under the pictures?

———————

———————

———————

———————

———————

———————

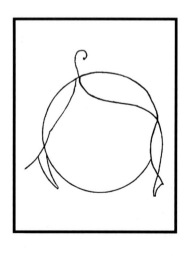

———————

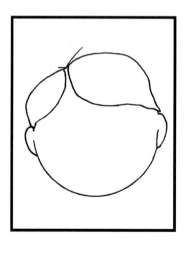

———————

How do you feel today?

Can you draw in the blank face how you feel today? Think of a good word for how you feel and write it underneath your drawing.

© 2001 Cath Smith.   May be copied for use by purchaser only.

IT'S NOT WHAT YOU SIGN - IT'S THE WAY THAT YOU SIGN IT!

The examples here show how the face can change the meaning of a sign. The pictures show a smiling or neutral face, then a questioning expression and one that you wouldn't want to argue with. The different meanings are quite clear from the face even though the sign is the same.

mine

mine?

mine!

alright

alright?

alright!

who?

someone

See how the face changes the meaning in these two signs to make 'who?' become 'someone' Get the picture?

© 2001 Cath Smith.   May be copied for use by purchaser only.

BSL HANDSHAPES

BSL makes use of approximately 22 major handshape 'groups' or 'families' which contain in total about 57 varients.

Most of these handshapes have a number of different functions as **'classifiers'**.

This means that they can be used to refer to actions, people or objects based on their *physical shape* or *outline*, or how they are *grasped, handled* and *moved*.

This is a fascinating area that may be featured in future publications, but is not the focus of this edition.

Let's Sign starts with 5 useful basic and commonly occurring handshapes. Signs with the same handshape are grouped together to help understanding and learning.

These handshapes have been chosen for their usefulness and simplicity of production, to help introduce students to one of the key building blocks of BSL. These can be added to and built on at various stages, as and when appropriate.

Throughout the book, they are referred to by the terms (from the top)

- **CLOSED HAND**
- **GOOD HAND**
- **POINTING HAND**
- **CLAWED HAND**
- **FLAT HAND**

They may be seen from different perspectives and orientations - like the examples here of the **POINTING HAND** shown palm forward and palm back.

The explanatory captions with the signs in the 'flashcard' section have been kept as simple as possible.

Fuller descriptions of movement and orientation are given in **'Tutor's Notes'** with each set of signs.

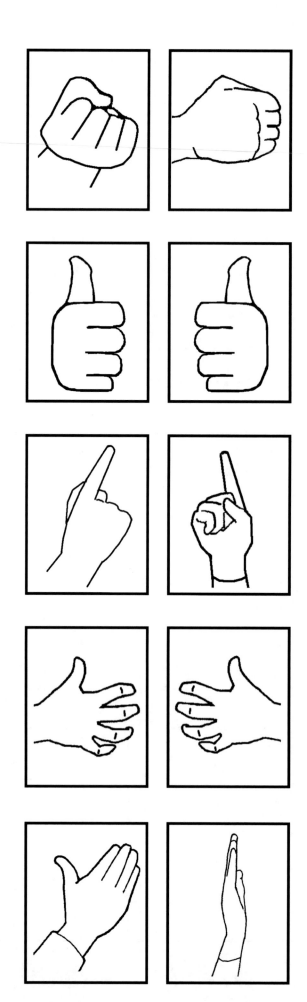

  © 2001 Cath Smith.   May be copied for use by purchaser only.

LOCATION and MOVEMENT: The Head - The Mind Area

The previous page on BSL handshapes, and the Tutor's Notes in the following pages explain more about handshapes and how they can be linked to meaning.

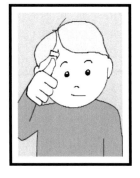

Another important feature is the **location** of that handshape on the *head* or *body*, and as we have already seen, this information is also combined with the face and bodily expression and **type** and **direction of the movement.**

It's useful to look in more detail at sign locations, and to group signs that occur in particular bodily locations together to see how these can be linked to meaning.

Most signs connected with *mental activity* are made on, or start from, the *forehead*, such as those grouped here.

The '*good*' hand with its *positive connotations* occurs in the top two signs, **KNOW** and **CLEVER** and the location on the forehead brings the implied meaning of knowledge, or understanding.

The movement in **CLEVER** can be sharp, with the cheeks puffed, a common intensifier in BSL to indicate '*brilliant*', '*very clever*' and so on.

In **THINK**, the index finger contacts the forehead. This can be a simple touch, or can move in small circles as illustrated, giving the idea of revolving ideas in the mind conveying such meanings as '*consider*' '*mull over*' and other words or phrases of similar meanings.

This version of **WORRY** is also sometimes located on the body, where the clawed hand (with its associations of tension) moves in repeated circular movements, inferring *stomach churning unease.* Located on the head, as it is with this group of signs, the idea of *mental turmoil, unease,* or a *troubled, anxious mind* seems to be very clearly portrayed.

DON'T KNOW is a good example of a negative sign with the flat hand touching the head, then moving down and away from the signer, combined with the negative features of *shrugged shoulders* and *head-shake.*

Positive statements can be changed to negative with a shake of the head and appropriate facial and bodily expression. Students can be encouraged to think about such changes in meaning as they work through the sign groups. For example, ask students how they might sign '*not me*', '*not yours*', '*not easy*', '*not pleased*' and so on.

A movement away from the signer occurs in some negatives, '*don't like*' is one example, and '*don't agree*' involves both '*good*' hands moving apart and opening (not illustrated).

© 2001 Cath Smith.   May be copied for use by purchaser only.

LOCATION and MOVEMENT: The Body - Feelings and Emotions

Signs that relate to *affections*, *physical* and *emotional feelings* and *behaviour* are most frequently located on the body.

FEEL involves the tip of the middle finger moving up the body, to convey feeling in both the physical and emotional senses. Both hands can be used for this sign, as illustrated in VARIATIONS.

The connection of the heart with *affections* and *feelings* is perhaps an obvious link, and may provide a rationale to this particular group of signs.

LIKE involves tapping the chest with a flat hand, and in **PLEASED** it moves in a circular rubbing movement, also meaning **HAPPY**. In some regions this means **SORRY**, or a closed hand is used as in the illustration here, but of course *context* and *appropriate expression* clarify meaning.

In **SAD** the flat hand moves down the body, conveying '*down hearted*' '*depressed*' and so on, and the accompanying facial and bodily expression reinforce this.

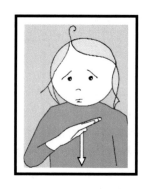 

This version of **WORRY** is also sometimes located on the head, where the clawed hand moves in repeated circular movements, inferring *mental turmoil* or *troubled mind*. Located on the body in this group of signs, the idea of *stomach churning unease* and *anxiety* seems to be very clear.

The clawed hand, with it's associations of *tension* or *agitation* occurs in the four remaining '*feeling*' signs here. In **JEALOUS** it is drawn across the chest, and in **SCARED** it makes small repeated contact with the chest as the face and body cower.

EXCITED involves a quick repeated alternate up and down rubbing movement and animated expression, whereas **ANGRY** involves a sharp and emphatic upward burst as both hands move upwards, apart and twist to palms up.

 © 2001 Cath Smith.   May be copied for use by purchaser only.

HANDSHAPE GROUP ONE: CLOSED HAND
Tutor's Notes

The first group of signs use a closed hand, or fist.

This is important in BSL in indicating *possession*, as in the first sign **HAVE**. The hand is palm up and open, closing firmly to a fist as the word is mouthed.

The closed hand is placed against the signer's chest to indicate **MY** or **MINE** and if twisted to face forward with slight movement, it indicates **YOUR** or **YOURS**.

This can be directed towards the relevant person, with eye-gaze in the same direction to indicate '*his*' '*hers*' and so on.

Eye-gaze is always important in indicating the person referred to.

The knuckles of the closed hand tap the chin twice in **NUMBER**, and this sign is also used to mean '*maths*'.

In **SORRY**, the lips are pressed together and the closed hand rubs in circular movements on the chest. The head may be tilted.

In some areas, the little finger is also extended or a flat hand is used (like our **PLEASED**) but *context* and *facial expression* should avoid confusion.

This is one variation of **HUNGRY** involving a small up and down rubbing movement on the stomach. **COLD** involves small in and out movements of the arms with the hands closed or in fists, and this sign is also used to mean '*winter*'.

In **BREAK** or **BROKEN**, the hands make the action of holding and snapping something, and **BROTHER** involves rubbing the knuckles of closed hands up and down against each other.

In **HELP** a closed hand rests on a flat hand and the hands move together in a small arc forward (as in "*I'll help*") or backwards (as in "*help me*") and is an example of a *directional verb* which changes direction to indicate the subject and object.

© 2001 Cath Smith. May be copied for use by purchaser only.

HANDSHAPE GROUP TWO: GOOD HAND
Tutor's Notes

In BSL, a closed hand with the thumb extended frequently occurs in signs that have pleasant or positive connotations. This is not always the case, but is a general principle that help learners understand and remember this group of signs. The convention of the 'thumbs up' for meaning 'OK' or 'good' is not universal, as is often thought, but does have this conventional association in BSL, and for convenience, in this book, is referred to as a 'good' hand.

(The sign **GOOD**, itself is in the 'chat signs' group of signs). The first example, **KNOW**, shown here involves touching the side of the forehead with the thumb tip of this 'good' hand and in **CLEVER** it moves sharply across the forehead. This forehead location is also linked to meaning, and is the most common location for signs connected with *mental activity*, described in more detail on page 23.

NICE involves the thumb being drawn from left to right across the chin, and can also mean 'lovely' 'sweet' or 'tasty'. In **USE** or **USEFUL**, the thumb makes a repeated small downward brushing movement on the chin.

ALRIGHT (or **ALL RIGHT**) is also used to mean 'fine', 'OK' and so on and both hands can be used at the same time in outward circular movements.

NEXT or **TURN** involves the hand twisting over from palm down to palm up, or can change direction, for example twisting back to the signer as in 'my turn'.

The small repeated contact in **BETTER** compared to the single sharp movement in **BEST** also seems to reflect the comparative aspect of 'better' compared to the superlative 'best', as well as match the syllables of the words.

In **AGREE** the 'good' hands move in to contact each other. This can also be signed with the lips pressed together as the head nods in 'agreement' which this sign also means.

In **HARD** or **PROBLEM** (also 'difficult') we see one of the exceptions to the positive aspects of the 'good' hand. The thumb tip prods the palm of the other hand and the cheeks may be puffed to show degree or intensity, as in 'rock hard', 'very difficult' and so on.

 © 2001 Cath Smith. May be copied for use by purchaser only.

HANDSHAPE GROUP THREE: POINTING HAND
Tutor's Notes

A closed hand with the index finger extended forms the basis of this group of signs, and for convenience is referred to as a *'pointing'* hand.

Pointing is part of BSL and is not considered rude in Deaf culture.

The tip of the extended index contacts the signer's chest to indicate **I** or **ME**, and points forward with eye-gaze towards the person being referred to in **YOU**. This can also be directed to other people to indicate *'him'*, *'her'* for example.

The signs **GIRL** and **BOY** have other variations that can be found in the VARIATIONS section.

The examples shown here use the side of the index finger making small forward brushing movements on the cheek in **GIRL.** In **BOY**, the extended index points and brushes right to left across the chin.

In this version of **WHO?** the index finger is moved in small horizontal circles (a neutral facial expression can change its meaning to *'someone'*). Another version is also illustrated in VARIATIONS.

The index pointing up makes small quick side to side movements with a questioning facial expression in **WHAT?**

From the same starting point, the hand makes a movement sideways in a small arc, meaning **AFTER** or **LATER**.

The forehead is the location for the index finger in the sign **THINK** which can also mean *'ponder'*, *'mull over'* and words of similar meaning.

The sign can be made by the index just tapping the forehead and also means *'sensible'*.

The index prods the cheek in **EASY** and the cheek may be puffed out to show intensity (eg *'dead easy'* *'doddle'*).

The sign **HEARING** refers to a *hearing person* and the index moves from the ear to the mouth or chin and may tap the chin twice.

© 2001 Cath Smith.   May be copied for use by purchaser only.

HANDSHAPE GROUP FOUR: CLAWED HAND
Tutor's Notes

Clawed hand

A hand with all the fingers extended and bent is referred to here as a 'clawed' hand.

The first sign shows this handshape making small circular movements in front of the mouth and means **WARM**.

The same handshape and location but with a sharp movement across the mouth gives the sign for **HOT** and in some areas is also used for 'summer'.

A clawed hand at the side of the chin (or head) with quick shaking movements to and fro means **MISTAKE** or **ACCIDENT** and is also a regional sign for 'sorry' (the shoulders should be raised in a gesture suggesting 'oops').

The clawed hand frequently appears in signs expressing *tension* or *agitation*. This version of **WORRY** involves a clawed hand making small circular movements near the side of the head, and is also sometimes located on the body, indicating *churned up emotions*, or *anxiety*.

Moving downwards in front of the face, it is used to express the idea of a long face as in **SULK** or **MISERABLE**. Tapping into the chest with a cowering expression, it means **SCARED**, **AFRAID** or 'frightened' and similar meanings.

The clawed hand is drawn across the heart in **JEALOUS** with appropriate facial expression, and the indication of *bad manners* is given in the quick up and down rubbing movements in **RUDE**.

EXCITED involves the fingertips of both clawed hands rubbing excitedly up and down in small alternate movements on the chest, and also means 'interested' 'keen' or 'eager'.

Facial expression is important in all of these signs, and the movement in **ANGRY** or **MAD** can also add to the idea of *blowing up*, of something explosive. The hands make a short, sharp movement up the body and twist at the wrists to finish palms up, and apart.

The cheeks may again be puffed to indicate intensity.

© 2001 Cath Smith.   May be copied for use by purchaser only.

HANDSHAPE GROUP FIVE: FLAT HAND
Tutor's Notes

The final handshape in the group is a *'flat'* hand in which the fingers are held straight and together.

The first sign shows a variation of **SCHOOL,** in which the flat hand is palm back in front of the mouth and makes small quick side to side movements (two other versions are given in VARIATIONS).

The fingers of a flat hand tap twice against the chin with the mouth slightly open as if stiffling a yawn in **BORED** or **BORING**.

With a slight movement to the right, this same handshape and movement indicate **BEFORE** or **PAST** and give an example of the use of forward and backward movements in BSL to indicate time in terms of *future* and *past.*

In this version of **THIRSTY** or **WATER** the fingertips of a flat hand making small downward brushing movements on the throat. There are a number of other variations (not shown).

In **LIKE**, the flat hand pats the chest twice with a positive facial expression to give the idea of enjoying or liking something, similar to **PLEASED** or **HAPPY** which uses a circular movement.

The flat hand moves forward and down from the forehead for **DON'T KNOW**, and with the *headshake* and *shrugged shoulders* gives a good example of **negation** in BSL (ask students how *'don't like'* may be signed?)

The same handshape and movement but starting from the mouth gives **PLEASE**, sometimes bending at the palm knuckle as it moves forward. Both hands can be used moving forwards and apart for **THANK YOU**.

The index edge of a flat hand rises up sharply to the middle of the forehead in **DANGER** and may tap the head twice. The eyes are open wide.

In **SAD**, the index edge of the flat hand moves down the body, as the *shoulders* and *face droop* to match the mood. In another version the flat hand moves down in front of the face, palm left.

© 2001 Cath Smith.   May be copied for use by purchaser only.

HANDSHAPE GROUP SIX: CHAT SIGNS
Tutor's Notes

The ten signs in this group do not fit into the selected handshapes, but are useful signs that have been added to enable some simple exchanges and conversations.

An obviously needed sign in a book such as this is **DEAF**, usually referring to a *born deaf sign language user.* The hand is closed with the index and middle fingers extended (an 'N' hand), and touching the ear. This can be further modified by puffed cheeks, as in *'profoundly deaf'* for example.

In **SIGN** the open hands rotate around each other and can also be modified to indicate, *'chat'*, *'talk non-stop'* and so on.

FINGERSPELL involves all the fingers wiggling against each other, and if this formation also moves to the right, it means *'to spell'* An 'N' hand is used again in **NAME** or **CALLED** where the fingers touch the forehead, then twist and move forward.

MUM or **MOTHER** and **DAD** or **FATHER** are examples of signs based on fingerspelt initials. In some regions the 'M' hand in *mother* is tapped against the forehead, but the version illustrated here is widely used and understood.

SISTER involves the bent index finger tapping the nose twice, and in **FEEL** the tip of the middle finger brushes upwards on the chest.

The *'good'* hand appears again in the sign **GOOD**, or **HELLO** when it is used as a greeting. This can be modified by facial expression to mean *'quite good'* *'great'* *'excellent'* and so on, and both hands can be used for emphasis.

These same principles apply to **BAD** where facial expression is also central to its meaning. In BSL this handshape occurs frequently in signs expressing unpleasant or negative ideas, like a counterpart to the *'good'* handshape. Bearing in mind the action of the *'good'* hands in **BETTER** and **BEST**, students may be able to work out how to apply the same principle to sign **WORSE** and **WORST**.

30

© 2001 Cath Smith.   May be copied for use by purchaser only.

VARIATIONS

Most of the signs used in BSL are standard and used and understood throughout the country. There is also wide variation in the use of some signs in a way that can be compared to accent and dialect in spoken language. Number systems and colours for example are subject to wide variation.

Variations may be due to geographical area and particularly school background, or may simply reflect individual choice and style. It is an area that causes a lot of anxiety to learners, but is just another aspect of the language that can be understood and learned.

The signs for **Let's Sign** are chosen in handshape groups. They are all widely used signs, but in some cases, they are not the only versions. This page, with the flash cards overleaf, show some other examples. Local Deaf contacts can advise you on signs used in your area. You may want to change some of the signs used in the sets for your own regional version.

These examples show regional signs for **GIRL** and **BOY**. Two variations of **SCHOOL** and another example of **WHO?** are illustrated here, although there are more.

ACCIDENT or **MISTAKE** shown here is located a little higher than the one used in the sets, and this type of small difference is common in some signs. **WORRY**, can be located on the body where it has meanings associated with *anxiety* and *unease* and even *queasiness*, illustrating that it is impossible to allocate single word for word translations between languages.

This version of **AFTER** is an alternative rather than a regional difference, as with **HELLO**, offering a different way of greeting. **FEEL** gives an example of a two handed sign that is also commonly signed with one hand, as in the sets. (**THANKYOU** is another example).

All natural languages change and develop with use, and new coinages. Differences in signs are only to be expected, in fact it would be much more surprising if sign variation did not occur and all signs were the same everywhere.

© 2001 Cath Smith.   May be copied for use by purchaser only.

girl

Move your 'pointing' finger left to right across your forehead.

boy

Brush the fingertips of your 'N' hand twice down your chin.

school

Hold your 'N' hand facing forward near your face, and shake it side to side.

© 2001 Cath Smith.   May be copied for use by purchaser only.

school

Tap the edge of your flat hand twice near your shoulder.

who?

Tap your 'pointing' finger twice on your chin. Look questioning.

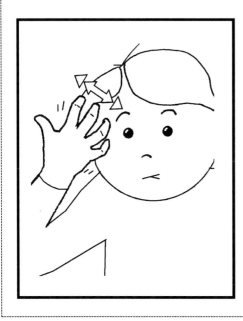

mistake or accident

Shake your 'clawed' hand near your head. Lift your shoulders.
Look sorry.

© 2001 Cath Smith.   May be copied for use by purchaser only.

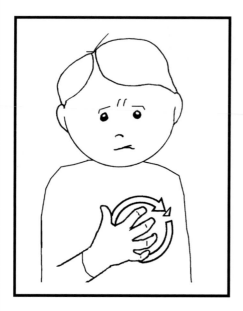

worry

Make small circles with your 'clawed' hand on your chest.
Look worried.

after

Twist your 'good' hand forward over your other hand.

hello

Make a small wave from the side of your head or in front of you.

© 2001 Cath Smith.   May be copied for use by purchaser only.

FINGERSPELLING AND ITS ROLE IN BSL

• Fingerspelling involves forming individual letters of the alphabet as illustrated, to spell out words in whole or in part.

• It is an important and integrated part of BSL, and is used is very specific ways.

• It is rarely used to spell out whole phrases or sentences (except by small numbers of older Deaf people who were taught by fingerspelling as children).

• It provides a direct link to literacy.

• It is commonly used to spell out names of people and places.

• It is used for some commonly occurring small words, that become recognised as signs eg 'DAY' 'IF'.

• Fluently spelt words are read as patterns.

• It uses abbreviated forms eg 'BHM' BIRMINGHAM.

• Repeated initials can become signs eg 'MM' MOTHER, 'KK' KITCHEN, 'TT' TOILET and so on.

• Repeated initials or abbreviated patterns are commonly used for days and months eg 'WW' WEDNESDAY, 'JAN' JANUARY and so on.

• It is used for acronyms eg 'NVQ' 'GCSE' 'BBC' 'NHS' and 'BSL'

• It can be integrated into a sign eg NAME, FAMILY.

• It is used more in some parts of the country than others.

• It is used more by some Deaf people than others.

• It is used more by older Deaf people.

• It can be quickly learned but needs lots of practice to read back words as patterns.

• It is best learned in word patterns and rhythms.

• BSL uses a two-handed fingerspelling alphabet.

• Australian Sign Language (Auslan) uses the same alphabet.

• Some sign languages use one-handed alphabets, eg Irish Sign Language, American Sign Language.

There are many different written alphabets and different forms of manual alphabets in existence throughout the world. Britain uses a two-handed system, but the majority of fingerspelling systems used by other countries are one-handed forms.

The individual letters in the alphabet shown in the illustrations can be compared with the written form of individual letters taught at primary school. Just as written letters change considerably when written fluently by hand, so fingerpelt letters alter considerably in fluent use. A similar ability to recognise words as 'patterns' also occurs in the fluent use of fingerpelling, as it does in the reading of written words.

Cut Out and Match the Fingerspelt Letters worksheets can be used at any stage, depending on when fingerspelling is introduced to students (see separate suggestions in Starting to Fingerspell).

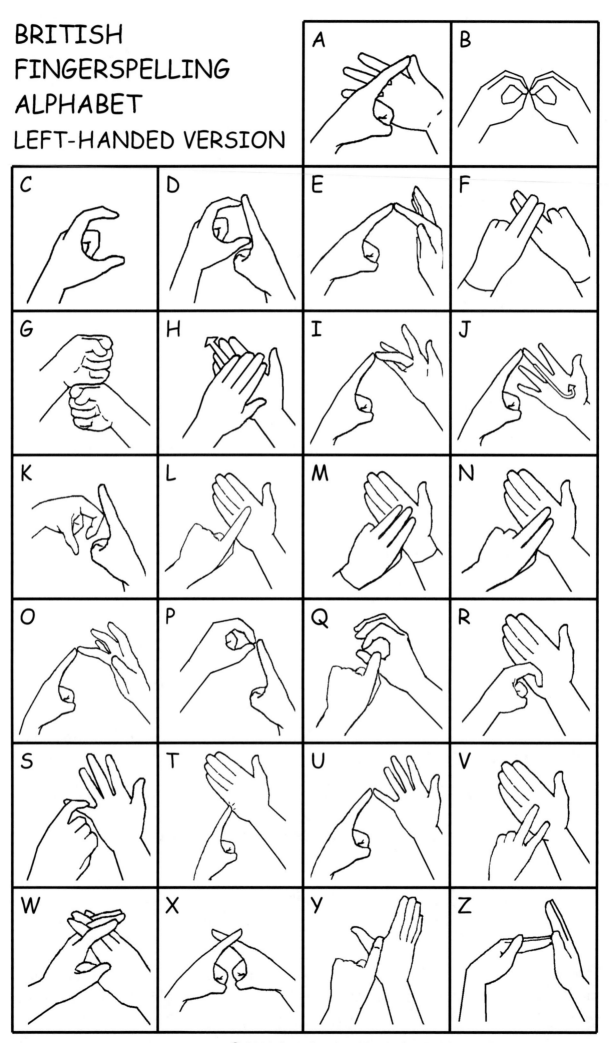

BRITISH
FINGERSPELLING
ALPHABET
LEFT-HANDED VERSION

 © 2001 Cath Smith.   May be copied for use by purchaser only.

BRITISH FINGERSPELLING ALPHABET
RIGHT-HANDED VERSION

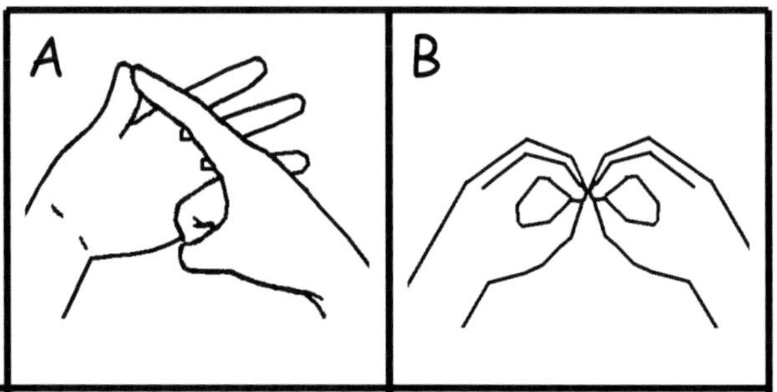

A

B

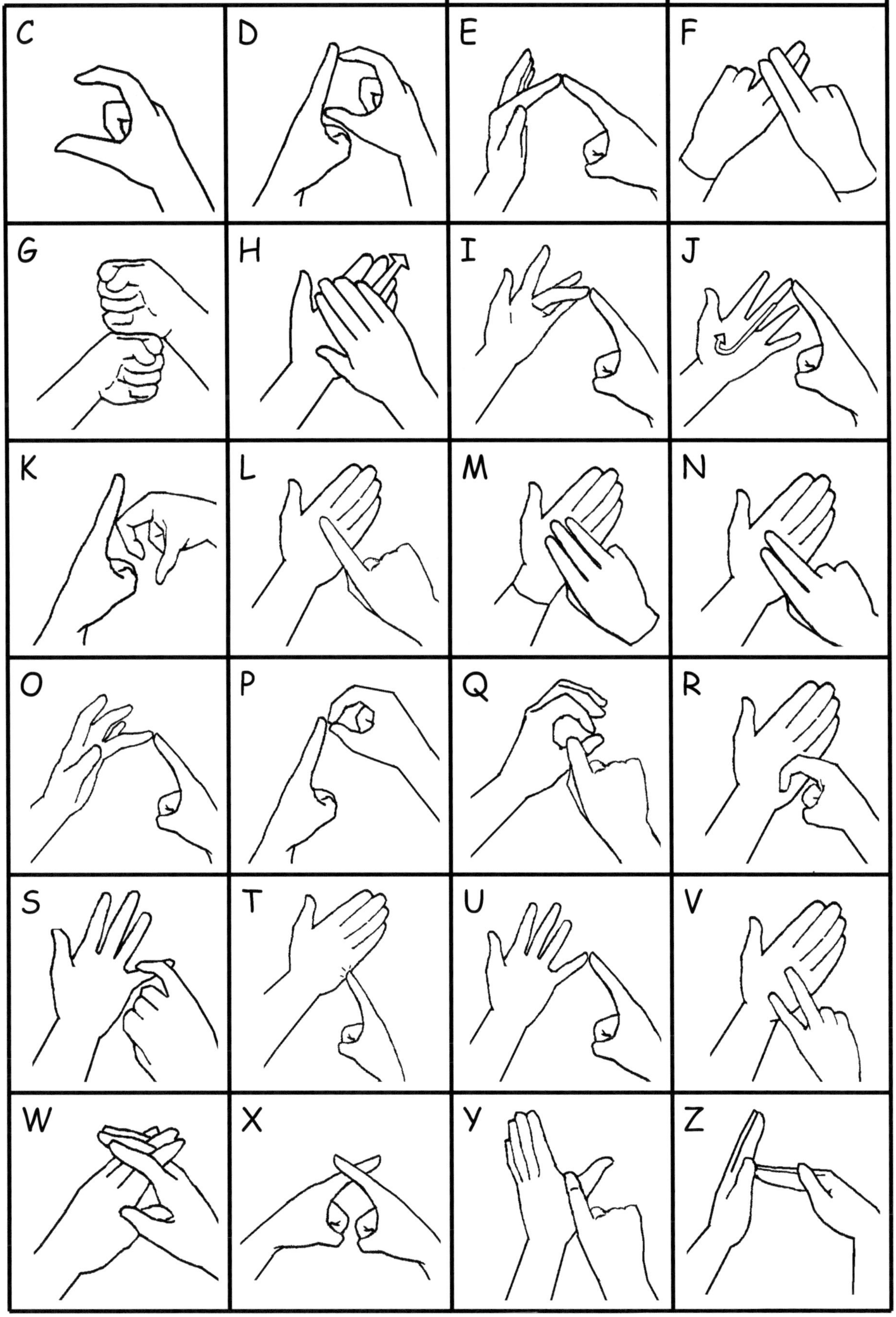

C

D

E

F

G

H

I

J

K

L

M

N

O

P

Q

R

S

T

U

V

W

X

Y

Z

© 2001 Cath Smith.   May be copied for use by purchaser only.

Starting To Fingerspell - Some Suggestions

Many BSL classes begin with fingerspelling as it can be learned very quickly and has so many uses, but some tutors recommend that it is introduced later, and in stages.   It really depends on the needs and abilities of the group.

A suggested way is to introduce groups of 5 or 6 letters at a time. This can be in alphabetical order, ABCDEF one week, then GHIJKL another week, and so on. This is the order used in the Cut Out and Match Fingerspelling worksheets which will ensure that all the letters have been covered and also reinforce the written form.

An even better way is to start with the students' names, before moving on to the worksheets. This develops the ability to see words as patterns, as with the written word, and can be made into a spelling practice game, using these letters.

For example, take the names **AMY** and **BEN** (or any other names from the student group). Write them on the board, or large sheet of paper so they can be seen.

Explain that you are going to learn how to spell them on your fingers.

Demonstrate the letters. Say the letters as you demonstrate them. Don't twist your hands to face the class, hold them loosely facing yourself as illustrated.

Ask the students to fingerspell the letters with you, and check that they are forming the letters correctly.

Students should use the same hand they write with as the dominant or moving hand. A right-handed and left-handed version of the Alphabet are illustrated.

After demonstrating, spell the names smoothly as you mouth the full names **AMY**, **BEN** without voice. Don't mouth the individual letters 'A' 'M' 'Y', 'B' 'E' 'N'.

Repeat several times, picking up speed and ask the students to do the same, you will feel a rhythm and pattern starting to emerge. **This is the key to fingerspelling**.

Ask the students to practice in pairs or small groups, without voice, mouthing the words as they spell them.

Ask the students to find how many 2 and 3 letter words can be made from the letters of the two names, eg AM, BE, MY taking turns of one spelling to the other. The words can be written down.

Remind the students to mouth the words, not the letters, whenever fingerspelling.

Only mouth individual letters if they are initials, for example **BSL**.

Depending on the group, this work can be extended and built on using a new and longer word at each session. Days of the week are also useful and give more letters to work from, or shorter words can be picked at random, depending on student's level. Words can be spelt out at various times of the day eg "Now its **PLAY** time" "it's **WET** outside" "**HOME** time" and so on.

Other word games such as 'Hangman' or any spelling practice sets, and word lists can be used for fingerspelling practice, and will help general spelling skills at the same time.   The picture Lotto sets can also be fingerspelt rather than signed. Students can take turns to call and mark and this is excellent practice for developing patterns and rhythm, both expressively and receptively.

For deaf children, fingerspelling has enormous potential for increasing vocabulary, enhancing lip-reading and developing literacy skills.

CUT OUT AND MATCH THE FINGERSPELT LETTERS

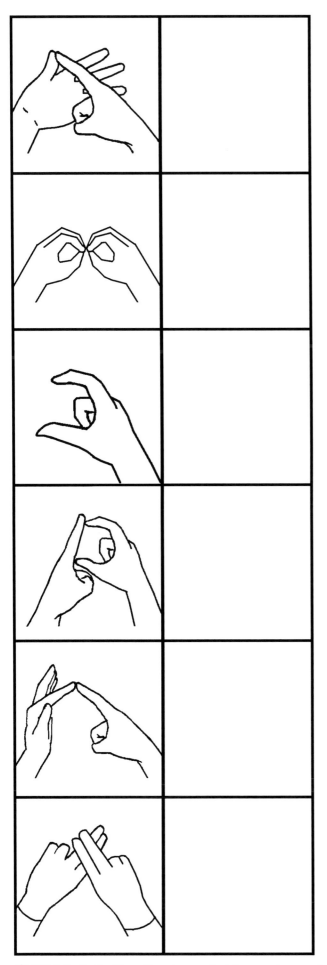

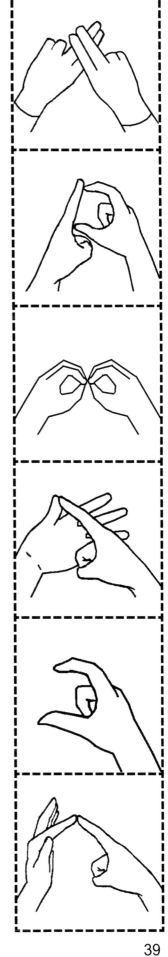

Cut these letters out, stick them in the right box and write the letter with it.

© 2001 Cath Smith.   May be copied for use by purchaser only.

CUT OUT AND MATCH THE FINGERSPELT LETTERS

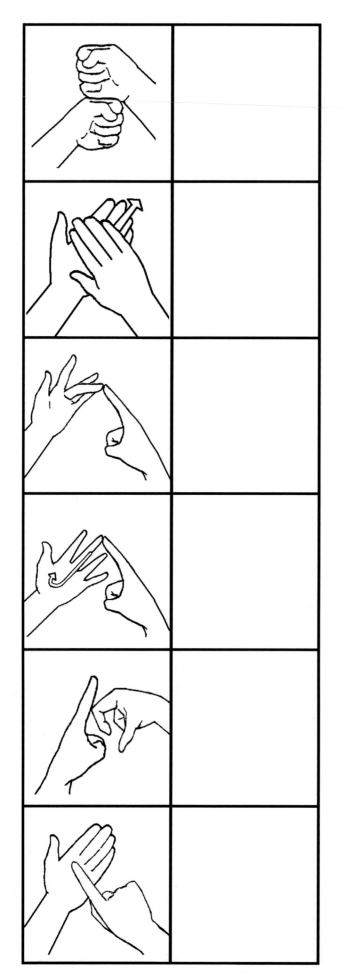

Cut these letters out, stick them in the right box and write the letter with it.

 © 2001 Cath Smith. May be copied for use by purchaser only.

CUT OUT AND MATCH THE FINGERSPELT LETTERS

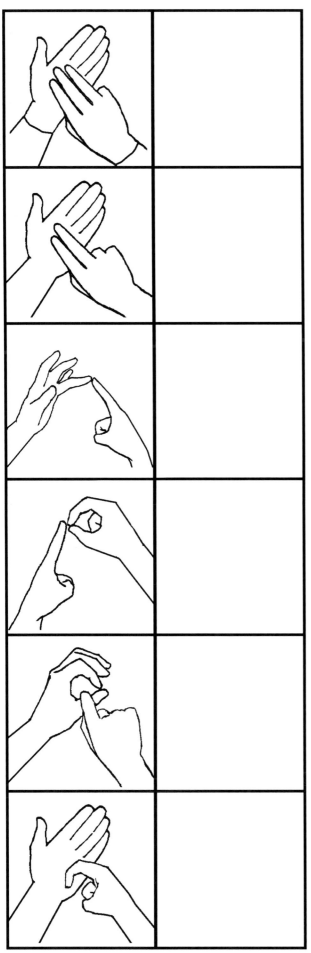

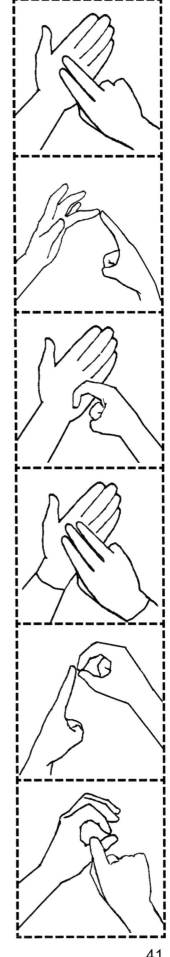

Cut these letters out, stick them in the right box and write the letter with it.

© 2001 Cath Smith.   May be copied for use by purchaser only.

CUT OUT AND MATCH THE FINGERSPELT LETTERS

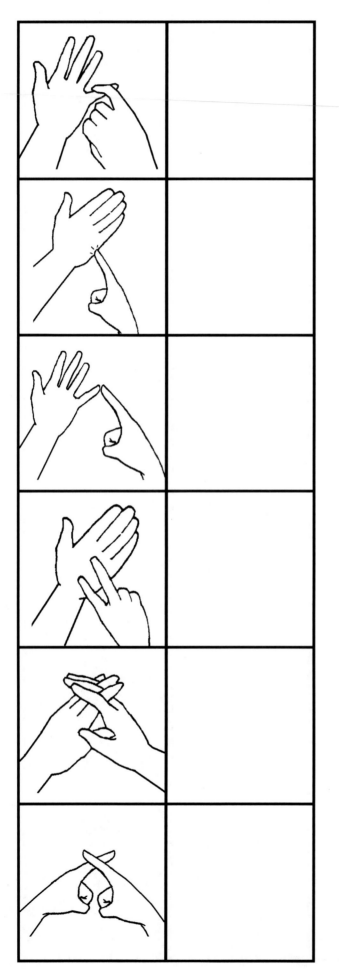

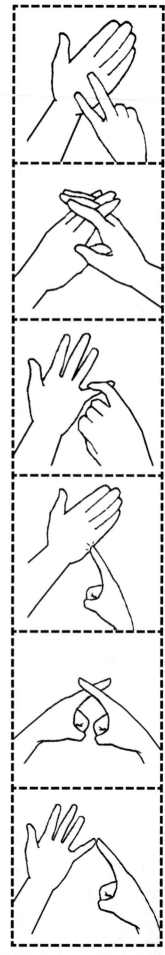

Cut these letters out, stick them in the right box and write the letter with it.

© 2001 Cath Smith.   May be copied for use by purchaser only.

CUT OUT AND MATCH THE FINGERSPELT LETTERS

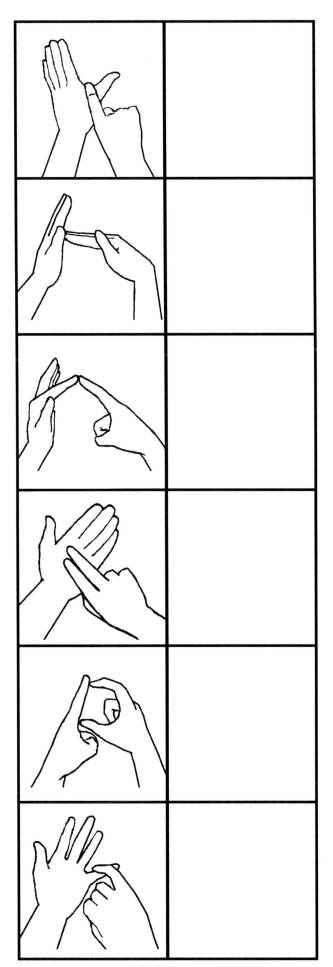

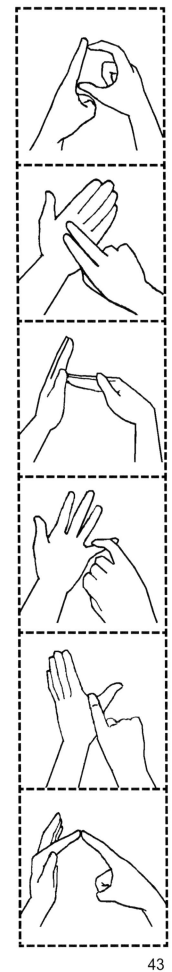

Cut these letters out, stick them in the right box and write the letter with it.

© 2001 Cath Smith.   May be copied for use by purchaser only.

INTRODUCING THE SIGNS
The Materials and Suggestions for Use

All of the materials in this section can be copied for class or homework. These are just some suggestions and you can probably think of more.

Some worksheets can be copied onto paper, and some of the exercises and games will work better if copied onto card and laminated for use with dry-wipe pens. Some sections are plain line drawings, and can be coloured before laminating.

Most local libraries and Post Offices now have copying facilities, for those who don't have access to school or college resources.

Some sections will work well if copied onto A3 sheets.

THE SIGN VOCABULARY

The Tutor's Notes section earlier in the book show each handshape group on one page. These can also be copied for handouts and the additional details relating to the signs can be explained to the group. **The materials in this section** begin with **flashcards** of the illustrated signs alongside simple explanations of the movements.

The English word translations are of the main meaning or meanings of each sign, but there is rarely a single word for word equivalent between languages. In some instances the ideas the sign represents can be signed a number of different ways. In others, the meaning of the sign covers a number of English translations.

Only one form of each word is usually given, such as *help*, rather than all possible translations such as *help, helps, helping, helped, helpful* or *mum, mummy, mam, mother*. Other signs can be modified as described in Tutor's notes to show intensity, to extend the meanings such as *bad, awful, terrible, horrendous* or *sad, depressed, down in the dumps* and so on. Only the main meaning of each sign is used in the worksheets and games.

FLASHCARDS

There are 3 signs to a page, and these can be copied and cut out as described above, keeping the caption and sign together. These can then be used as flash cards to introduce the signs in the handshape groups (see Tutor's Notes) 5 or 10 at a time depending on the group. The chat signs can be integrated at any stage.

- Show the card and demonstrate the sign, as you say the word.
- Draw attention to the facial expressions and bodily movements.
- Ask the students to sign it with you and check that they are doing it correctly.
- All the drawings are right handed, but left handed students will use their left hand.
- Repeat several times whilst mouthing the word without voice.
- Work through the 5 or 10 signs in the handshape group.
- Run through all 5 or 10 to show that it is the same handshape changing locations.
- The students can practice in pairs or small groups, without voice.
- Show the cards with the sign hidden and ask students to say the word.
- Show the cards with the word hidden and ask students to sign it without voice.
- Copy two sets and use for 'memory' or 'snap' or other matching games.

SIGN/WORD CARDS TO MATCH

Each page is made up of one of the handshape groups of signs plus 2 *chat signs*, to make up 12 to a page. The words then follow in the same sequence. Since they will be cut up, the *chat signs* can be kept as a separate section if preferred.

These cards can be used to reinforce learning after each handshape group has been introduced, and are useful for homework. They can be coloured.

Suggestions for use

* Copy onto card and **cut out each sign box and each word box**. Mix up and ask students to match the signs and words.

* Spread the **sign** cards face up. Ask students to try to remember them, then turn them face down. Make one of the signs, or fingerspell one of the words. Students take turns to turn over a card to find the sign.

* Repeat using the **word** cards.

* Turn sign and word cards face down. Students turn over to find matching pairs.

* Deal out the **word** cards. Students can work in pairs or small groups to fingerspell their words to the others. The first student to 'get it' makes the sign, then spells out their word.

* Students work in pairs or small groups. One side has the signs, the other has the words. Without speaking, one side asks the other for either a sign or word to match what they have by signing "have you......?" and signing what they need. The matching word and sign can be put down side by side.

* Use two sets of signs, or word cards, turn face down. Students take turns to turn two over to find matching pairs. They must make the sign when they turn it over.

* Alternatively, the word pages can be kept as one sheet, and students match the sign by placing them over the word.

* Give students a set of pictures to stick in their book and write the word.

When all the signs have been worked through, they can be put in simple combinations for students to write out, then read back, eg **'MY MUM' 'YOUR BROTHER' 'AFTER SCHOOL' 'I DON'T KNOW'**.

The word cards can be sorted into words of 2, 3, 4 letters and so on and used for fingerspelling practice and games.

Link the Handshapes to the Signs worksheets help students to tune in to recognising handshapes, and this exercise can be done before the signs have been learned. The last page of these worksheets uses the handshapes from the signs in VARIATIONS.

Circle the Right Word and **Link the Words and Signs** worksheets are set out in the handshape groups. They can be used as worksheets for class or home following the introduction of each handshape group, or in later sessions as revision. Copy onto paper or onto laminated card for use with dry-wipe pens for re-use.

PICTURE LOTTO

The first set of six Lotto 'cards' are set out in the handshape and 'chat signs' groups. (these can make useful little reference sets or memory aids at any stage). The second set of six cards are mixed - the last one contains all the signs from VARIATIONS. They have a different format to distinguish them, although all 12 'cards' can be used for Lotto games.

Different permutations can be made by simply cutting each card in half across the middle and pasting with a different half for larger groups of students.

The Sign/Word Cards can be used for 'calling'. Simply shuffle them, then pick one at a time. The 'caller' makes the sign (and mouths the word without voice) to the group, who check their card and either mark with a pen, or cover with a counter. The four corner signs only can be used for quick games, or single line, or 'full house'.

- The winner can be the next caller.

- Games can be played with signs or fingerspelling, or a combination of the two.

- Clues can be given to the signs by adding the fingerspelt initial.

When all the sign groups have been completed, the following materials can be used, although the signs for the dominoes can be taught first if preferred for younger children and for family games.

PICTURE DOMINOES

These need to be copied onto card if possible, and A3 card would be better for younger children, to make bigger cards.

When copied, write on the back 'Set One' and 'Set Two' and 'Set Three' in case they get mixed up.

The signs for each set are;

SET ONE
ME, YOU, MUM, DAD, BOY, GIRL, WHO?

SET TWO
MINE, YOUR, EASY, HARD, GOOD, BAD, WHAT?

SET THREE
HAVE, KNOW, NAME, SIGN, LIKE, FEEL, NEXT

Encourage students to make the signs when they lay a domino, and use signs such as '*me next*' '*your turn*' and so on.

Fill in the Missing Letters spelling exercises are graded on the number of letters in the English translations, so also involve a mixture from different groups and are best used when all the signs have been worked through.

INDEX

Makes a useful record sheet. As the signs are learned, they can be ticked off, or coloured in.

have

Close your hand like holding something.

mine or my

Close your hand and hold it on your chest.

your or yours

Hold your closed hand forward towards the person you mean and look at them.

   © 2001 Cath Smith.   May be copied for use by purchaser only.

number

Tap your knuckles on your chin twice.

sorry

Rub your closed hand in circles on your chest. Look sorry.

hungry

Rub your closed hand up and down on your tum.

© 2001 Cath Smith.   May be copied for use by purchaser only.

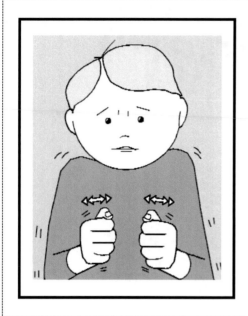

cold

Move your closed hands in and out like shivering. Hunch your shoulders.

break or broken

Move your closed hands like snapping something.

brother

Rub the knuckles of your closed hands together.

 © 2001 Cath Smith. May be copied for use by purchaser only.

help

Rest your closed hand on your flat hand and move them forward or back to yourself.

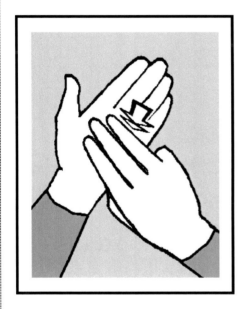

mum or

mother

Tap your 'M' hand on your flat hand twice.

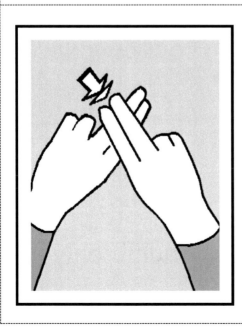

dad or

father

Tap your right fingers twice on top of your left.

© 2001 Cath Smith.   May be copied for use by purchaser only.

good or hello

Hold your 'good' hand in front of you. Look pleased.

bad

Close your hand with the little finger sticking up. Move it forward, and frown.

know

Make a 'good' hand and touch your thumb on your forehead.

 © 2001 Cath Smith.   May be copied for use by purchaser only.

clever

Make a 'good' hand and brush your thumb across your forehead.

nice

Make a 'good' hand and brush your thumb across your chin. Look pleased.

use or
useful

Brush your thumb twice down the middle of your chin.

© 2001 Cath Smith.   May be copied for use by purchaser only.

alright

'Good' hand moves round in a circle.

next or turn

Make a 'good' hand and twist it over.

better

Make two 'good' hands. Brush one thumb forward against the other, twice.

 © 2001 Cath Smith.   May be copied for use by purchaser only.

best

Make two 'good' hands. Bang one thumb forward against the other, once.

agree

Make two 'good' hands and bring them together.

hard or

problem

Make a 'good' hand and prod your other hand twice with your thumb.

© 2001 Cath Smith.   May be copied for use by purchaser only.

I or me

Point your finger to yourself.

you

Look at the person you mean and point to them.

girl

Brush your 'pointing' finger forward twice on your cheek.

© 2001 Cath Smith.   May be copied for use by purchaser only.

boy

Brush your 'pointing' finger to the left across your chin.

who?

Make small circles with your finger pointing up. Look puzzled.

what?

Shake your 'pointing' finger side to side in front of you. Look questioning.

© 2001 Cath Smith.   May be copied for use by purchaser only.

after or

later

Hold 'pointing' hand up in front of you. Move it sideways away from you.

think

Touch your forehead with your 'pointing' finger, and make a small circle.

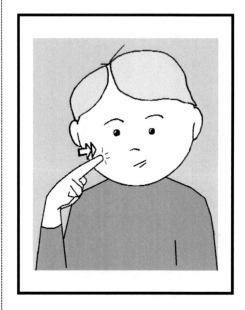

easy

Puff your cheeks and prod twice with your 'pointing' finger.

 © 2001 Cath Smith. May be copied for use by purchaser only.

hearing

Move your 'pointing' finger from your ear to your mouth.

deaf

Make an 'N' hand and touch your ear.

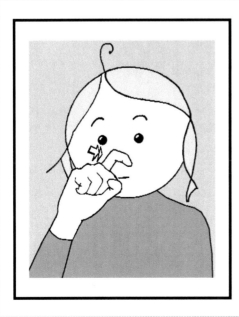

sister

Bend your 'pointing' finger and tap it twice on your nose.

© 2001 Cath Smith.   May be copied for use by purchaser only.

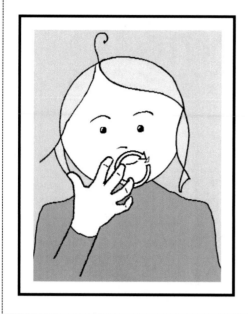

warm

Move your 'clawed' hand in small circles in front of your mouth.

hot

Move your 'clawed' hand sharply across near your mouth.

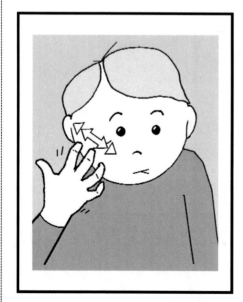

mistake or accident

Shake your 'clawed' hand near your face. Lift your shoulders. Look sorry.

© 2001 Cath Smith.   May be copied for use by purchaser only.

worry

Make small circles with your 'clawed' hand near your head. Look worried.

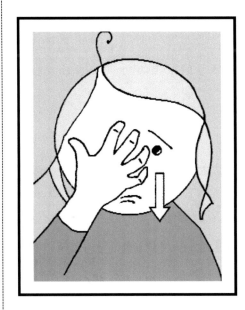

sulk or

miserable

Drag your 'clawed' hand down in front of your face. Look miserable.

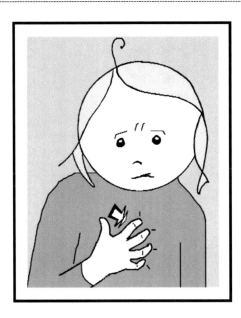

scared or

afraid

Tap your fingers twice on your chest. Hunch your shoulders and look scared.

© 2001 Cath Smith. May be copied for use by purchaser only.

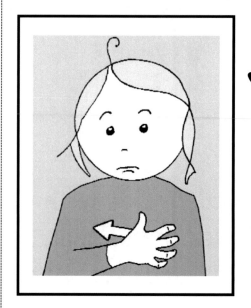

jealous

Drag your 'clawed' hand across your chest.

rude

Rub your 'clawed' hand fingertips up and down on your arm. Look cross.

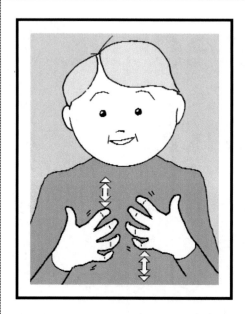

excited

Rub your 'clawed' hand fingertips up and down on your chest, alternately. Look excited.

 © 2001 Cath Smith.   May be copied for use by purchaser only.

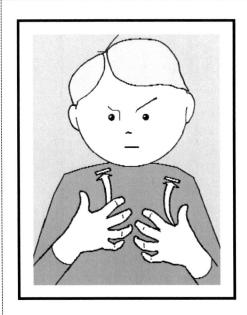

angry or
mad

Move both 'clawed' hands sharply up your body. Look mad.

feel

Move your middle finger up your body.

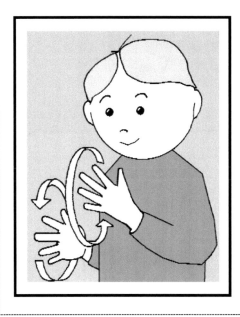

sign

Move your open hands in alternate forward circles.

© 2001 Cath Smith.   May be copied for use by purchaser only.

school

Shake your flat hand side to side in front of your mouth.

bored or boring

Tap your flat hand on your chin twice (like yawning). Look bored.

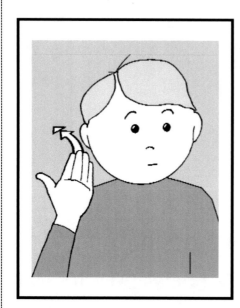

before or past

Wave your flat hand backwards over your shoulder.

© 2001 Cath Smith. May be copied for use by purchaser only.

thirsty or
water

Brush the fingertips of your flat hand down your neck, twice.

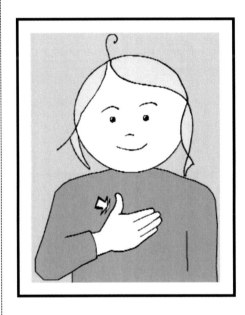

like

Tap your flat hand twice on your chest.   Look pleased.

pleased or
happy

Rub your flat hand in circles on your chest. Look happy.

© 2001 Cath Smith.   May be copied for use by purchaser only.

don't know

Touch your forehead with your hand, and move it forward and down, as you shake your head and shrug.

please or thank you

Move your flat hand forward and down from your mouth.

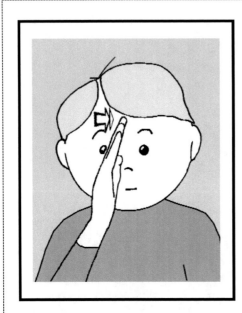

danger

Bring the edge of your flat hand sharply up to the centre of your forehead.

 © 2001 Cath Smith.   May be copied for use by purchaser only.

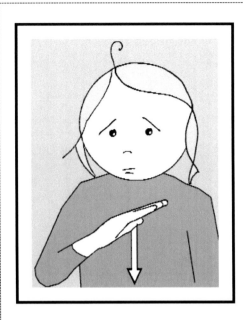

sad

Turn your flat hand to face down. Move it down your body. Look sad.

name or
called

Make an 'N' hand. Touch your forehead and twist it forward and down.

fingerspell

Wiggle all your fingers against each other.

© 2001 Cath Smith. May be copied for use by purchaser only.

SIGN/WORD CARDS TO MATCH

© 2001 Cath Smith.   May be copied for use by purchaser only.

WORD/SIGN CARDS TO MATCH

have	mine	your
number	sorry	hungry
cold	break	brother
help	mum	dad

© 2001 Cath Smith.   May be copied for use by purchaser only.

SIGN/WORD CARDS TO MATCH

 © 2001 Cath Smith.   May be copied for use by purchaser only.

WORD/SIGN CARDS TO MATCH

good	bad	know
clever	nice	use
alright	next	better
best	agree	hard

© 2001 Cath Smith.   May be copied for use by purchaser only.

SIGN/WORD CARDS TO MATCH

 © 2001 Cath Smith.   May be copied for use by purchaser only.

WORD/SIGN CARDS TO MATCH

me	you	girl
boy	who?	what?
after	think	easy
hearing	deaf	sister

© 2001 Cath Smith.   May be copied for use by purchaser only.

SIGN/WORD CARDS TO MATCH

 © 2001 Cath Smith.   May be copied for use by purchaser only.

warm	hot	mistake
worry	sulk	scared
jealous	rude	excited
angry	feel	sign

© 2001 Cath Smith.   May be copied for use by purchaser only.

SIGN/WORD CARDS TO MATCH

© 2001 Cath Smith.   May be copied for use by purchaser only.

school	bored	before
thirsty	like	pleased
don't know	please	danger
sad	name	finger-spell

© 2001 Cath Smith.   May be copied for use by purchaser only.

LINK THE HANDSHAPES TO THE SIGNS

 © 2001 Cath Smith. May be copied for use by purchaser only.

LINK THE HANDSHAPES TO THE SIGNS

© 2001 Cath Smith. May be copied for use by purchaser only.

LINK THE HANDSHAPES TO THE SIGNS

© 2001 Cath Smith.   May be copied for use by purchaser only.

LINK THE HANDSHAPES TO THE SIGNS

LINK THE HANDSHAPES TO THE SIGNS

© 2001 Cath Smith.   May be copied for use by purchaser only.

LINK THE HANDSHAPES TO THE SIGNS

© 2001 Cath Smith.   May be copied for use by purchaser only.

CIRCLE THE RIGHT WORD

	mine your number have sorry
	your have sorry number mine
	number mine your have sorry
	sorry number mine your have
	mine your have sorry number

© 2001 Cath Smith. May be copied for use by purchaser only.

CIRCLE THE RIGHT WORD

	cold help break brother hungry
	help hungry brother break cold
	hungry brother cold help break
	cold break hungry brother help
	brother hungry help cold break

© 2001 Cath Smith.   May be copied for use by purchaser only.

CIRCLE THE RIGHT WORD

	use clever nice know alright
	alright use know nice clever
	use nice know alright clever
	use alright clever nice know
	know use alright clever nice

86

© 2001 Cath Smith. May be copied for use by purchaser only.

CIRCLE THE RIGHT WORD

	better agree hard best next
	best next agree better hard
	hard better best agree next
	agree best better hard next
	better hard next agree best

© 2001 Cath Smith.   May be copied for use by purchaser only.

CIRCLE THE RIGHT WORD

	girl me you boy who?
	who? girl boy you me
	girl boy who? me you
	you me girl boy who?
	girl you me who? boy

© 2001 Cath Smith. May be copied for use by purchaser only.

CIRCLE THE RIGHT WORD

	think hearing easy what? after
	hearing what? after easy think
	what? easy hearing think after
	easy after think hearing what?
	after think what? easy hearing

© 2001 Cath Smith.   May be copied for use by purchaser only.

CIRCLE THE RIGHT WORD

	hot warm worry mistake sulk
	sulk hot mistake warm worry
	worry mistake warm sulk hot
	mistake sulk hot warm worry
	worry warm sulk hot mistake

  © 2001 Cath Smith.   May be copied for use by purchaser only.

CIRCLE THE RIGHT WORD

	rude jealous scared excited angry
	jealous scared angry rude excited
	scared angry excited jealous rude
	angry excited rude scared jealous
	excited rude jealous angry scared

© 2001 Cath Smith.   May be copied for use by purchaser only.

CIRCLE THE RIGHT WORD

	like thirsty before bored school
	before school bored thirsty like
	thirsty before school like bored
	bored before like school thirsty
	school bored thirsty before like

© 2001 Cath Smith. May be copied for use by purchaser only.

CIRCLE THE RIGHT WORD

	don't know sad danger please pleased
	pleased don't know please sad danger
	danger please pleased sad don't know
	please danger don't know pleased sad
	danger pleased sad don't know please

© 2001 Cath Smith.   May be copied for use by purchaser only.

CIRCLE THE RIGHT WORD

	sign deaf feel good bad
	good feel sign bad deaf
	deaf sign bad feel good
	feel bad deaf good sign
	deaf feel good sign bad

© 2001 Cath Smith. May be copied for use by purchaser only.

CIRCLE THE RIGHT WORD

	mum sister dad name fingerspell
	sister name fingerspell dad mum
	dad sister mum fingerspell name
	mum fingerspell sister name dad
	fingerspell dad name mum sister

© 2001 Cath Smith.   May be copied for use by purchaser only.

LINK THE WORDS AND SIGNS

my

brother   have

your   sorry

number

hungry

break

help

cold

    © 2001 Cath Smith.   May be copied for use by purchaser only.

LINK THE WORDS AND SIGNS

best

agree   alright

nice   use

next   hard

know   clever

better

© 2001 Cath Smith.   May be copied for use by purchaser only.

97

LINK THE WORDS AND SIGNS

you

what?

after

who?

boy

girl

hearing

easy

me

think

© 2001 Cath Smith.   May be copied for use by purchaser only.

LINK THE WORDS AND SIGNS

mistake

jealous

hot

sulk

warm

scared

excited

angry

rude

worry

© 2001 Cath Smith.   May be copied for use by purchaser only.

99

LINK THE WORDS AND SIGNS

before

danger

sad

thirsty

bored

please

don't know

like

school

pleased

© 2001 Cath Smith. May be copied for use by purchaser only.

LINK THE WORDS AND SIGNS

deaf

dad

sister

good

name

bad

mum

sign

feel

spell

© 2001 Cath Smith.   May be copied for use by purchaser only.

PICTURE LOTTO CARD

have	mine	your	number	sorry
hungry	cold	break	brother	help

PICTURE LOTTO CARD

know	clever	nice	use	alright
next	better	best	agree	hard

 © 2001 Cath Smith. May be copied for use by purchaser only.

PICTURE LOTTO CARD

me	you	girl	boy	who?
what?	after	think	easy	hearing

PICTURE LOTTO CARD

warm	hot	mistake	worry	sulk
scared	jealous	rude	excited	angry

© 2001 Cath Smith. May be copied for use by purchaser only.

PICTURE LOTTO CARD

school	bored	before	thirsty	like
pleased	don't know	please	danger	sad

PICTURE LOTTO CARD

deaf	sign	fingerspell	name	mum
dad	sister	feel	good	bad

 © 2001 Cath Smith.   May be copied for use by purchaser only.

PICTURE LOTTO CARD

warm	school	good	mine	bad
me	you	warm	have	bored

PICTURE LOTTO CARD

number	your	who?	know	thirsty
boy	worry	before	clever	mistake

© 2001 Cath Smith.   May be copied for use by purchaser only.

PICTURE LOTTO CARD

use	pleased	sulk	nice	girl
sorry	like	what?	hungry	scared

PICTURE LOTTO CARD

jealous	alright	sad	after	think
rude	best	please	break	cold

 © 2001 Cath Smith.   May be copied for use by purchaser only.

PICTURE LOTTO CARD

better	easy	excited	don't know	help
next	hearing	danger	angry	brother

PICTURE LOTTO CARD - VARIATIONS

school	boy	girl	school	who?
mistake	worry	after	hello	feel

© 2001 Cath Smith.   May be copied for use by purchaser only.

PICTURE DOMINOES SET ONE

 © 2001 Cath Smith. May be copied for use by purchaser only.

© 2001 Cath Smith.   May be copied for use by purchaser only.

PICTURE DOMINOES SET TWO

© 2001 Cath Smith.   May be copied for use by purchaser only.

© 2001 Cath Smith. May be copied for use by purchaser only.

111

© 2001 Cath Smith.   May be copied for use by purchaser only.

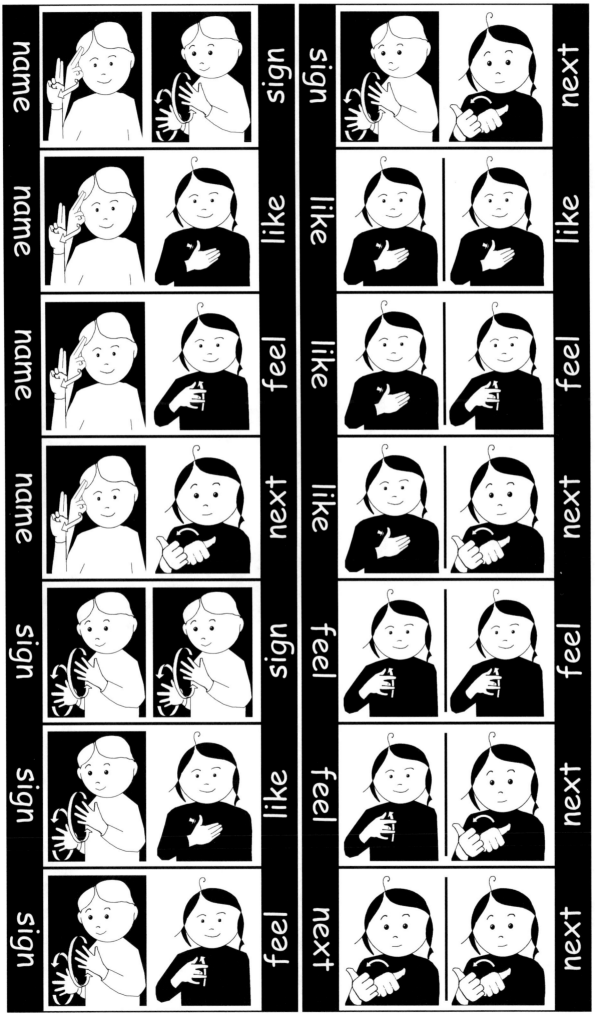

© 2001 Cath Smith.   May be copied for use by purchaser only.

FILL IN THE MISSING LETTERS

m _

m _

b _ _

b _ _

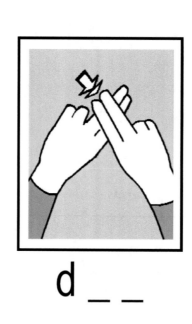

d _ _

h _ _

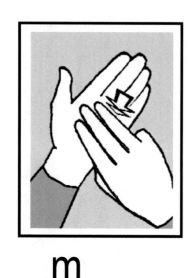

m _ _

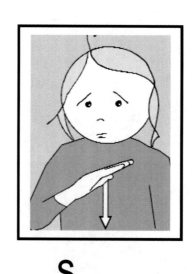

s _ _

u _ _

  © 2001 Cath Smith. May be copied for use by purchaser only.

FILL IN THE MISSING LETTERS

w _ _ ?

y _ _

b _ _ _

c _ _ d

d _ _ f

e _ _ y

f _ _ l

g _ _ l

h _ _ d

© 2001 Cath Smith.   May be copied for use by purchaser only.

FILL IN THE MISSING LETTERS

h _ _ e

h _ _ p

k _ _ w

l _ _ _

n _ _ _

n _ _ _

r _ _ _

s _ _ _

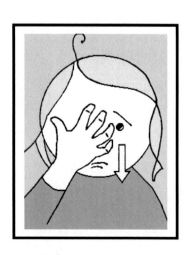

s _ _ _

   © 2001 Cath Smith.   May be copied for use by purchaser only.

FILL IN THE MISSING LETTERS

w _ _ _

w _ _ _ ?

y _ _ _

a _ _ _ r

a _ _ _ e

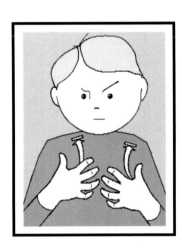

a _ _ _ y

b _ _ _ _

b _ _ _ _

s _ _ _ _

© 2001 Cath Smith.   May be copied for use by purchaser only.

APPENDICES
Sources and Recommended Reading

The LET'S SIGN Series of Resources: Co-Sign Communications. (See details and images page 127)

British Deaf Association (1992). Dictionary of British Sign Language/English. London: Faber and Faber.

Centre for Deaf Studies University of Bristol Research Notes 1: Language Development in School.

Conrad, R. (1979). The Deaf Schoolchild: Language and Cognitive Function. London: Harper & Row.

Hindley, Dr P. (Consultant Child and Adolescent Psychiatrist). Mental Health Services for Deaf Children. London: Young Minds Magazine Mar/Apr 1998 Issue No 33.

Klima, E. and Bellugi, U. (1979). The Signs of Language. Harvard University Press.

J. Kyle and H. Sutherland (1993). Deaf Children at Home. Centre for Deaf Studies, University of Bristol.

Pamela Knight, Ruth Swanwick (1999). The Care and Education of a Deaf Child: A Book for Parents. (Parents' and Teachers' Guides). Multilingual Matters.

Issues in Deaf Education. Susan Gregory (Editor), Stephen Powers (Editor), Linda Watson (Editor), Pamela Knight (Editor), Wendy McCracken (Editor) (1998). David Fulton Publishers.

M. Pickersgill & Dr S. Gregory (1998). Sign Bilingualism: A Model.

C. Smith (2002). Sign Language Link: a pocket dictionary of signs 3rd Edition. Co-Sign Communications: Stockton on Tees.

All above publications are available from Forest Books (details in Useful Contacts).

The National Deaf Children's Society (NDCS) Publications

The National Deaf Children's Society (NDCS) provide a range of helpful publications for parents and professionals on communication, education, audiology, technology and welfare benefits. Most publications are free of charge to parents of deaf children and available on-line from www.ndcs.org.uk

Omnidirectory 2. NDCS (2003). A comprehensive guide to deafness related technology, organisations, contacts and local services such as deaf schools, hearing impaired and social services.

Sign Language and Your Deaf Child. NDCS (2002). Practical information for parents thinking about using sign language with their deaf child. Includes around 60 basic family signs. Free to parents of deaf children.

Deaf Friendly Schools: A guide for teachers & governors. NDCS (2002). A guide for staff in mainstream schools who have a deaf child in their schools (secondary or primary). Information on teaching strategies, inclusion, communication, deafness and technical support. For parents and teachers.

Deaf Friendly Nurseries and Pre-Schools. NDCS (2003). Practical information for people working with deaf children under 5 in a mainstream nursery or pre-school setting.

Useful Contacts

(V) indicates a voice line, and (T) a text line

British Deaf Association (BDA)
1-3 Worship Street, London EC2A 2AB.
Tel: 020 7588 3520
Textphone: 020 7588 3529
Fax: 020 7588 3527
Helpline Textphone: 0800 652 2965
Helpline Telephone: 0870 770 3300
e-mail: helpline@bda.org.uk
web: www.bda.org.uk

Council for the Advancement of
Communication with Deaf People (CACDP)
Durham University Science Park, Block 4, Stockton Road, Durham DH1 3UZ.
Tel: 0191 383 1155 (V/T) **Text:** 0191 383 7915
Fax: 0191 383 7914
e-mail: durham@cacdp.org.uk
web: www.cacdp.org.uk

Deafsign.com
(British Sign Language Information and Resources)
16 Highfield Crescent, Hartburn,Stockton on Tees TS18 5HH.
Tel: 01642 580505 (V/T)
Fax: 01642 808959
e-mail: cath@deafsign.com
web: www.deafsign.com

Forest Books
(Specialists in Books, Videos, CD-Roms on sign language/deaf issues)
The New Building, Ellwood Road, Milkwall, Coleford, Gloucestershire GL16 7LE.
Tel: 01594 833858 (V/T)
Videophone: 01594 810637
Fax: 01594 833446
e-mail: forest@forestbooks.com
Web shopping site: www.ForestBooks.com

The National Deaf Children's Society (NDCS)
National Office 15 Dufferin Street, London EC1Y 8UR.
Freephone Helpline:
Mon-Fri 10 am - 5 pm 0808 800 8880 (V/T)
Fax: 020 7251 5020
Switchboard Tel: 020 7490 8656 (V/T)
e-mail: helpline@ndcs.org.uk
web: www.ndcs.org.uk

The Royal National Institute for Deaf People (RNID)
19-23 Featherstone Street, London EC1Y 8SL.
Tel: 020 7296 8000 (V) 020 7296 8001 (T)
Fax: 020 7296 8199
Information line:
Tel: 0808 808 0123 (freephone)
Textphone: 0808 808 9000 (freephone)
e-mail: informationline@rnid.org.uk
web: www.rnid.org.uk

Sign Bilingual Consortium of Schools and Services
Contact: Karen Simpson, Headteacher,
Frank Barnes Primary School for Deaf Children,
(Beacon School for Sign Bilingualism)
Harley Road,
London NW3 3BN.
Tel: 020 7586 4665
e-mail: admin@fbarnes.camden.sch.uk

BRITISH TWO-HANDED FINGERSPELLING ALPHABET

 © 2001 Cath Smith. May be copied for use by purchaser only.

INDEX - Glossary of Sign Entries with Descriptions

accident 60	alright 54	better 54
afraid 61	angry 63	bored/ing 64
after 58	bad 52	boy 57
after 34	before 64	boy 32
agree 55	best 55	break 50

© 2001 Cath Smith.   May be copied for use by purchaser only.

INDEX - Glossary of Sign Entries with Descriptions

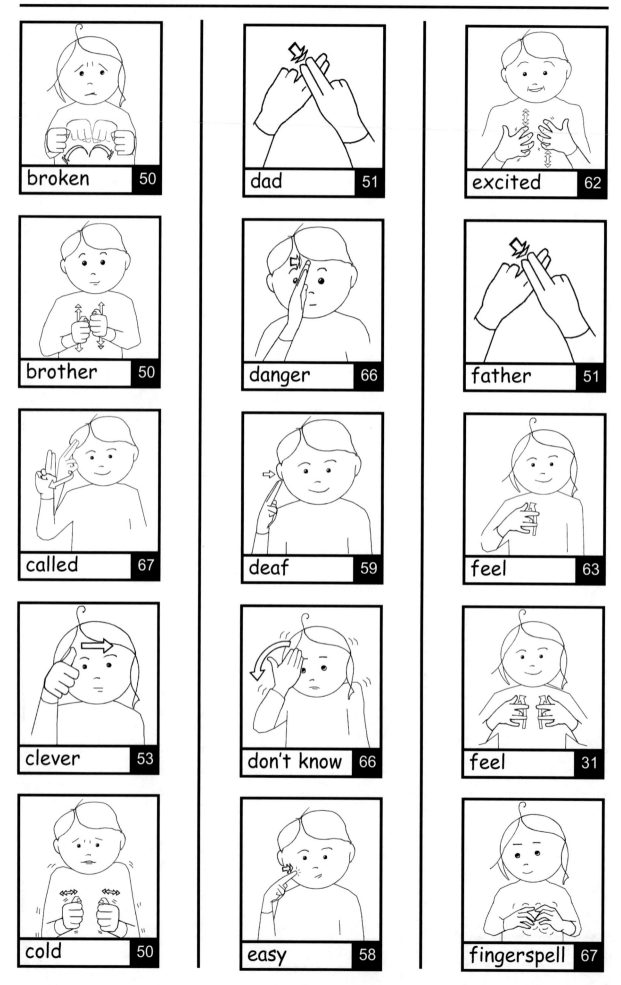

broken 50	dad 51	excited 62
brother 50	danger 66	father 51
called 67	deaf 59	feel 63
clever 53	don't know 66	feel 31
cold 50	easy 58	fingerspell 67

© 2001 Cath Smith. May be copied for use by purchaser only.

girl 56	have 48	hot 60
girl 32	hearing 59	hungry 49
good 52	hello 52	I 56
happy 65	hello 34	jealous 62
hard 55	help 51	know 52

© 2001 Cath Smith.   May be copied for use by purchaser only.

INDEX - Glossary of Sign Entries with Descriptions

later 58	miserable 61	my 48
like 65	mistake 60	name 67
mad 63	mistake 33	next 54
me 56	mother 51	nice 53
mine 48	mum 51	number 49

© 2001 Cath Smith.   May be copied for use by purchaser only.

INDEX - Glossary of Sign Entries with Descriptions

past 64	sad 67	sign 63
please 66	scared 61	sister 59
pleased 65	school 64	someone 21
problem 55	school 33	sorry 49
rude 62	school 32	sulk 61

© 2001 Cath Smith.   May be copied for use by purchaser only.

INDEX - Glossary of Sign Entries with Descriptions

thank you 66	useful 53	who? 33
think 58	warm 60	worry 61
thirsty 65	water 65	worry 34
turn 54	what? 57	you 56
use 53	who? 57	your/yours 48

© 2001 Cath Smith.   May be copied for use by purchaser only.

THE LET'S SIGN SERIES
Of British Sign Language Resources

A Deaf and hearing development committed to raising the status and profile of BSL through learning and teaching materials for all ages and abilities.

(Compatible with all educational sign systems based on British Sign Language)

Bold and eye-catching

A2 Poster

BSL and Deaf Awareness raising in Nurseries, Schools, Colleges, Hospitals and all Public Buildings.

Suitable for anywhere and everywhere.

German Sign Language version available

Colourful wipe-clean and in topics

A4 poster/mats

Greetings-Family
Feelings-Questions.

Other topics can be added on request.

Also available in Bengali and Gujarati
·Translations to other languages can be considered.

Let's Sign: For Work
BSL Guide for
Service Providers

The Disability Discrimination Act requires those providing services to take positve steps to improve access. For Deaf people this can be access to information and communication with agency staff.

* Over 170 appropriate signs
* Regional variations
* Clear communication advice and background
* Captions to describe how the sign is made
* Left and Right handed Fingerspelling Alphabets
* Useful Contacts and full Index

Suitable for all those whose work may bring contact with Deaf people.

Let's Sign: Early Years
Child and Carer Guide

Specially written introduction to signing by Deaf and hearing co-writers for early childhood communication and language development through British Sign Language (BSL).

* Over 300 everyday child appropriate signs
* Numerous regional variations
* Examples of signed phrases
* Numbers up to ten
* Captions to describe how the sign is made
* Left and Right handed Fingerspelling Alphabets
* Useful Contacts and full Index

Suitable for families and all those whose work brings contact with young children from babyhood onwards - deaf children, children with special needs and Baby Signing with hearing children.

LET'S SIGN: BSL Building Blocks
Taster Pack

Introduction to British Sign Language
for Beginners

6 basic lessons, copyable worksheets,
games and activities

A4 Tutor, A5 Student Primer and CD-Rom
of Deaf family demonstrating the signs.
(Items also available separately)

Let's Sign & Write
BSL Graphics for Sign Bilingual Material
Cath Smith/ Widgit Software

Create your own tailor-made resources
with over 700 sign graphics in line
drawings and colour.
Includes numerous regional variations.
To support signers, their peers, teaching and
care staff and families.

NGfL | National Grid for Learning

See our full range of
resources on our
National Grid for Learning
approved site

www.deafsign.com

British Sign Language Information and Resources
Full contact details page 123